freedom from
PROCRASTINATION

LIVING JOYFULLY AND PRODUCTIVELY
WITH GOD'S HELP

BARB RAVELING

Truthway Press
Copyright ©2019 Barb Raveling

Cover Design by Cindy Kiple
Interior Design by Cindy Kiple
Editing by Tracey Nicole Hayes, JHwriting+

ISBN 978-0-9802243-7-5

TABLE OF CONTENTS

*Use these resources throughout the five weeks to develop the habit of making
and finishing a realistic to-do list each day*

*When you feel like procrastinating, choose a renewing activity based
on your reason for not wanting to do the next thing on your list*

It's Not Important

INTRODUCTION

Let's face it. Most of us procrastinate something. It may be difficult projects. Relationships. Exercise. Decisions. Scary goals. Or maybe even your daily to-do list. You make it—but you rarely complete it. Or maybe you're like I used to be—you don't even bother making a list because you know you won't complete it.

Whatever the area you procrastinate, there's hope for you in this book. We'll go to God for help with the things we don't want to do—both through Bible study and also through various renewing of the mind activities you can use in the heat of the moment when everything in you wants to say, "No! I don't want to do that! I'll just do it later!!"

If you're a true-blue procrastinator, you may want to use this book to develop a habit of making and finishing a to-do list each day. If you're already in the habit of making and following a list each day, you could use this book to work on a more complicated goal or project—something you're scared to do or feel like you can't do.

No matter what you decide to work on, my prayer is that God will give you some victory with procrastination as you go through this study. Overcoming procrastination is a step-by-step project, so one Bible study won't cure all of your procrastination woes. But we can make great progress in five weeks. After all, we serve a powerful God and He is able to change us! Shall we begin?

HOW TO USE THIS BOOK

BIBLE STUDIES: Each week we'll cover a different reason for procrastinating. As you see how people like Jonah, Moses, and Jesus approached the things they didn't feel like doing, you'll learn lessons that will change the way you approach work and help you break free from procrastination.

TO-DO LISTS: Each day during the five weeks of this study, you'll make a to-do list, listing the three most important things you need to get done that day. I'll ask you to put at least one thing on the list that you dread doing so you'll have an opportunity to go to God for help with your to-do list.

RENEWING ACTIVITIES: After you make your list for the day, look at the first item on your list. If you can make yourself do it, go ahead and do it. If you can't make yourself do it, renew your mind with one of the renewing activities in the renewing section of this book. Think of this as a time to talk with God about your dreaded to-do. Your conversation will be based on your reason for wanting to procrastinate. For example, if you look at the next task on your list and think, *I don't want to do that,* turn to the Table of Contents and choose a renewing activity under the "I Don't Want to Do It" section. As you renew your mind, you'll usually find your desires changing. Often, I'll feel like doing my dreaded to-do halfway through the renewing activity. If that happens for you, go ahead and do your task; you don't need to finish the renewing activity.

ACCOUNTABILITY CHARTS: One of the hardest things about to-do lists is making yourself do them day after day, especially if you have lots of days when you don't complete the tasks on your list. The accountability charts are set up on a weekly basis so they'll motivate you to keep plugging away, even when you experience failure. They'll also help you remember to 1) make realistic lists based on time estimates, 2) prioritize your tasks, 3) renew your mind when you can't do the next task on the list, and 4) celebrate the tasks you've completed each day.

INDIVIDUALS AND GROUPS: This is a Bible study you can do on your own but it's also fun to do with a group as it's exciting to see God working in the lives of others to help them break free from procrastination. If you're leading a group, look for a leader's guide and introductory video at barbraveling. com/procrastination.

BIBLE STUDIES

Week One

IT'S NOT THAT IMPORTANT

Do you ever feel like you have a million things to do, but you're not doing any of them? Do you make a to-do list and then promptly lose it or ignore it? Do you suspect you'll never get caught up? If so, then you know what I've felt like for most of my life.

Procrastination runs deep in my bones and although the circumstances have changed depending on my stage of life, the chaotic consequences have remained the same. Take for example a typical day back when I was homeschooling our four young kids.

I'd begin the day by making breakfast for the kids, then clean up the kitchen while they scurried off to do their chores and get school started. I then spent the rest of the day lounging around the house, answering the occasional homeschool question, but mostly just doing whatever I felt like doing.

I had a sky-high stack of paperwork teetering on the edge of my desk, overflowing closets, an out-of-control yard and garden, and countless things I *could* do—but instead I did nothing. Not only could I not drum up the oomph to do the things I *should* do, I also didn't do the things I wanted to do.

What I wanted was fun and excitement, but the life of a homeschool mom wasn't all that fun and exciting. I loved my kids and thoroughly enjoyed them—but I would rather have been out camping and hiking with them than cooped up in a house doing schoolwork with them.

Thankfully, God began to change me in radical ways. First, He helped me dip my toes in the waters of doing-hard-things, and then He brought me along in a step-by-step process of overcoming procrastination. I'm not at the end of the road yet, but far enough along to enjoy the getting-things-done scenery.

If you're reading this book, I'm guessing you've had similar struggles. Maybe you're like the old me, where you hate the idea of work. You'd rather live a life of fun and indulgence, but the complications of that lifestyle—a disaster of a house, a spouse who isn't happy with your carefree ways, or always rushing around last minute to meet deadlines—have persuaded you to try this Bible study.

Or maybe you're more like the ten-years-ago me. You actually do some things you don't want to do. You have a to-do list you sometimes follow, yet you still procrastinate enough that it deeply affects the quality of your life and how much you can accomplish.

Or maybe you're like the current me. You have a list of projects and you're fairly productive. But you still feel overwhelmed because you don't know how to manage all your projects, and that often leads to procrastination.

Or maybe you can't relate to me at all because you're an on-the-ball person by nature. You like getting things done and checking them off your list. You don't struggle with procrastination, but you do have a scary goal in mind that you'd like some help with.

No matter where you are on the procrastination spectrum, this book will help. First, we'll join together to study God's Word and get a biblical perspective of work and productivity. Then we'll learn some practical productivity skills and practice those with weekly real-life work assignments. Finally, we'll work on developing a daily renewing-the-mind habit so we can follow through with our to-do lists even when every bone in our body is yelling, "Just let me sit down in my cozy chair and read my book! I don't want to do that crummy job on my list!!" Let's begin our journey by seeing what the Bible has to say about work and productivity.

1. Read the following verses. What can you learn about God's attitude towards work and productivity from each passage?

   a. Genesis 2:15

   b. Mark 10:42–45

   c. 1 Corinthians 15:58

   d. Ephesians 2:10

   e. Ephesians 5:15–16

   f. 2 Thessalonians 3:11–12

2. In summary, what do these verses teach about work and productivity?

3. Now think of your own attitude toward work and productivity. How is it different than God's attitude about work and productivity?

I don't know about you, but I was completely convicted by those Bible verses. Too often, I harbor an I-shouldn't-have-to-suffer attitude about work that causes me to sit back and procrastinate rather than get up and do the things God wants me to do.

It would be nice if I could just read those Bible verses and say, "Oh, the Bible says I should work. I guess I better stop procrastinating," then go my merry way, never struggling with procrastination again.

Unfortunately, that's not how change takes place.

Instead, it goes a little more like this: We get all excited about achieving some goal. We read up on it. We make a plan. We work on it enthusiastically for a week or two. Then one day we wake up without an ounce of motivation in our bodies. We decide to take a day off. The next day we're busy. We don't have time to work on our goal, so we take another day off. The following day we're tired, and the day after that we just don't feel like it. Before long our minds are headed to I'm-Such-a-Failure Land because we haven't worked on our goal in weeks. That's when the thoughts come in: *Who am I kidding? I'll never be able to do this! Why bother even trying?*

Then we close up the book (or in this case the Bible study) that's supposed to help us change, set it on the shelf, and forget about it until the next time we clean the bookshelf—which for us procrastinators, could be years!

We may *want* to change. We just don't have the self-control to make it happen. We're not the only ones who have experienced this phenomenon. Let's look at another person who knows what we're going through.

4. Read Romans 7:18–19. What was Paul's experience with having enough self-control to make himself do the things he knew he should do?

Can you relate to Paul? I can. I've wanted to change my procrastinating ways my whole life, but even now, I often find myself *not* doing the things I want to do (getting my work done or pursuing a goal) and instead doing the things I don't want to do (wasting time in various ways). My guess is that you know what I'm talking about. It would be easy to beat ourselves up and say, "I'm such a slug! I'll never be an on-the-ball person!" Thankfully, we don't need to do that.

5. According to Romans 8:1, why can we stop beating ourselves up about being such procrastinators?

6. It's wonderful to know that God doesn't condemn us when we fail, but if we're not careful, a misunderstanding of His grace can lead us into thinking we don't need to change. We might say, "This is just my personality. I can't change who I am." Do the following Bible verses support the idea that God doesn't care if we ever change? Explain.

a. Galatians 5:13

b. 1 Peter 1:14–16

God gives grace, but He also wants us to be holy so we can grow in our love for Him and others. There's a fine line to walk between holiness and grace. We don't want to fall on the side of the line that says we need to earn God's favor, but we also don't want to fall on the side of the line that says we have no responsibility to mature in Christ and grow in the area of our weaknesses—one of those weaknesses being procrastination.

7. Think of your own life in the area of getting things done. Which side of the line do you tend to lean toward: "I need to be super productive to be acceptable" or "I'm good enough as is—I don't need to change"? How does that side of the line affect the following?

a. Your personal wellbeing

b. Your productivity

c. Your relationship with God

d. Your relationship with others

8. Do you think God wants you to move more toward the middle of the line? If so, why?

9. How would your life change if you were to move closer to the middle of the line?

These last few questions are helpful to ask because they'll come up as you work on breaking free from procrastination. If you tend to focus on performance, you might condemn yourself when you don't follow through on your projects and goals. That could make you want to give up because you feel like such a failure.

If you're more freedom-oriented, you might feel like it's not a big deal if you gain victory over procrastination. You'll be tempted to give up when things get difficult because why bother when it's so much work?

Thankfully, God can take us where we are, speak truth into our lives, and help us persevere no matter what our tendencies. This Bible study is all about going to God for help with procrastination. We'll grow closer to Him as we lean on Him for help. Let's begin by seeing what the Bible has to say about the transformation process.

10. Read Romans 12:2. How does Paul say we're transformed?

So often we think we need to pull ourselves up by our bootstraps and just get a little more discipline in our lives. Enough of this messing around! But the truth is, we're not capable of changing in our own strength. Paul knows this because he tried it (Romans 7:18–19). Instead, Paul tells us to renew our minds if we want to be transformed. This is true for anything we want to change, including overcoming procrastination.

Renewing the mind involves two different things: 1) studying the Bible to see what it has to say about the area we're trying to change, and 2) going to God for help in the midst of transformation to *remember* what we learned in the Bible and see our current struggle from a biblical perspective.

The five Bible studies in this book will help with that first step, but we also need help with the second step. The second half of the book will help with the second step. **Take a minute now to glance through the hands-on section of this book.** You'll find to-do lists, accountability charts, and renewing-the-mind activities. These activities will help you take what you learn in the Bible and apply it right away in making and following your to-do lists each day.

During the Bible studies, you'll be learning biblical truths from the safety of your armchair. But in the hands-on section, you'll be counseling with the Holy Spirit in the heat of the battle. You'll be visiting with Him each day as you try—once again—to do what you *plan* to do rather than what you feel like doing. That's hard because we're trying to change behavior that's gone on for years or maybe even a lifetime. We need God's help.

We also need help with practical skills because overcoming procrastination is both a spiritual and a practical pursuit. Yes, we need to renew our minds if we want to be transformed, but we also need to learn some practical skills to become more productive. At the end of each Bible study, you'll find some practical productivity tips that tie into that week's lesson. You can also find podcast episodes and videos with tips on overcoming procrastination at barbraveling.com/procrastination. Let's get to this week's tips.

—❧ Weekly Productivity Tips ❧—

1. **Do difficult tasks when you have the most energy.** I'm guessing you already know what time of day you have the most energy. Try to schedule the tasks you dread for that time of day because that's when you'll be most likely to make yourself do them. I'm a morning person, so I schedule my difficult tasks in the morning. When I save them for the afternoon (translation: when I procrastinate), I almost always end up not doing them because I don't have enough energy in the afternoon to make myself do those tasks. One of the books that has really helped me with this concept is called *Deep Work* by Cal Newport. In the book, Cal talks about deep work and shallow work. Deep work is the work that requires mental concentration. I also label it as the work that is emotionally difficult to make yourself do because you dread it so much. Shallow work takes less concentration and is easy to make yourself do. Each day I have a deep work and shallow work focus, usually two hours for each. For me, writing a book is deep work because it involves mental concentration and it's a bit draining. Coaching is shal-

low work because it's fun and energizing. Having a deep and shallow work focus for the day helps me to mentally divide the day into two parts: deep work and shallow work. This helps me to get my difficult things done in the morning, but it also helps me avoid the discouragement that comes from trying to make myself do deep work in the afternoon when I'm pretty much incapable of doing deep work.

2. **Make a realistic to-do list and estimate how long each task will take.** Often I'll think, *Oh, this job will be so easy, I can do it in no time*. This procrastination study is a good example. I made an announcement to teach it at my church when I had an overall book plan but not one chapter written. I thought, *Oh, that won't be a problem since I already have an outline!* Well of course it was a problem! I got more discouraged than I needed to be about how hard it was to write because I wasn't realistic about how long it would take. Since then, I've begun estimating the amount of time I think a task will take to complete. This helps me avoid discouragement and an attack of the I-can't-do-this blues!

3. **Ask, "Why am I procrastinating?"** Sometimes just knowing why we're procrastinating will help us to stop procrastinating. If you find yourself reluctant to work on your project or to-do list, stop for a minute and ask, "Why am I procrastinating?" It might be because the job is too hard or maybe it's boring or maybe you don't know how to do it. Knowing why you're procrastinating will help you know what to do to start working on it. Just don't answer the question with, "Because I'm lazybones!"

4. **Ask, "What's the first step?"** Often, we don't feel like working because we see the whole project before our eyes and it's so overwhelming, we don't want to do it. If we instead ask, "What's the first step?" and focus *only* on that step, the project will seem less intimidating and we'll be able to make ourselves do it. Here's an example. This morning I had just finished my quiet time and knew I needed to go to my desk and start working on writing this study. I was procrastinating because I was so cozy in my chair, so I asked myself, "What's the first step?" My answer was "Take this blanket off my lap." Taking the blanket off my lap was much easier than writing the Bible study so I was able to do that step easily. Once I had the blanket off, it was easy to get out of the chair and walk to my desk to start writing. So yes, that sounds pathetic, but after all, I'm a procrastinator—I need to do what I can do!

—๑ *The Next Step* ๑—

Are you ready to start the hands-on portion of this study? Let's begin by finishing our first to-do list together! Complete the items on the following list and check them off when you have each item completed.

TASK	TIME ESTIMATE	COMPLETED
Watch the video "Intro to Freedom from Procrastination" at barbraveling.com/procrastination. If you don't have access to the Internet, review "How to Use This Book" on page 7 and look at the sample to-do list and accountability chart on page 154.	10 minutes	
Turn to page 62 and make your first to-do list. If possible, prioritize your list so that you begin with your most dreaded task.	5 minutes	
Turn to the Table of Contents and choose a renewing activity based on your reason for dreading the first task on your to-do list. Answer the questions with your dreaded to-do in mind, and then get started on your first to-do!	15 minutes	

Record your progress by signing your name on one of the three lines below:

1. I completed the above to-do list. Yay!!!!

_____

2. I wanted to complete it but I couldn't make myself do it, so I'm now headed into the second Bible study. But that's okay—I'm a work in progress and God will change me as I continue to go to Him for help with procrastination!

_____

3. I thought that seemed like too much work, so I skipped doing all of those things, and I'm now headed into the second Bible study. But that's okay—I'm a work in progress and God will change me as I continue to go to Him for help with procrastination!

⁓ঌ *Moving On* ঌ⁓

From this point forward, you'll be mixing Bible study with hands-on to-do list practice. If you're doing this with a class, you'll do one Bible study and 5-6 to-do lists and renewing activities per week. You can either work your way through the renewing activities in the order given or choose an activity based on the reason you don't feel like doing the next thing on your list.

If you're doing this study on your own, you can work through the Bible studies more quickly if you'd like. Don't feel like you have to do a whole Bible study in one day. Depending on your time and concentration, you may want to take several days to work through one of the studies. I'm excited to see what God will do in your life as you go to Him for daily help with overcoming procrastination!

Week Two

I DON'T WANT TO DO IT

When I was in college, I would procrastinate all of my studying until the last possible minute because I found most of the textbooks super boring. I would far rather have fun with my friends than crack a book. Because of this, I'd be forced to stay up late the night before a test cramming a month of learning into several hours. Fortified with treats from the dorm vending machines, I'd tackle those books and end up with an okay grade.

I was a big fan of fun and easy in those days, and studying wasn't fun. Fast forward a few years, and I approached housework the same way—put it off until the last possible minute because it wasn't fun. Paperwork? Put it off until the last minute because it wasn't fun. Weight loss? Put if off until the last minute because it wasn't fun. Any type of boring work? Put it off until the last possible minute because it wasn't fun.

This went on for another 25 years past college until, thankfully, God intervened. He has taught me how to work even when I don't feel like working and also how to actually enjoy work. I'll never be a Type A person (and that's okay), but I am becoming a competent person—and that feels good.

If you're doing this study, I'm guessing you can relate. You know what it's like to look a job in the face and think, *Nah, I think I'll do something fun instead.* We're not the only ones who escape when we have unpleasant jobs. In today's lesson we'll talk about another person who was in the habit of doing whatever he felt like doing.

1. Read Jonah 1:1–3. What did God ask Jonah to do and why do you think He wanted someone to do that task for Him?

2. How did Jonah respond to God's request?

3. Why do you think Jonah chose to do what he felt like doing rather than what God wanted him to do?

Have you ever felt like Jonah, where you didn't want to do something God wanted you to do? Jonah probably would have been happy to see the Ninevites destroyed because they were the Israelites' enemies. Yet God asked Jonah to warn them because God loved the Ninevites, and He wanted to show His love for them through Jonah.

It's easy to look at Jonah's response and think, *Wow. I can't believe he flat out turned down God. That's so terrible!* But don't we do the same thing sometimes when we procrastinate on our to-do lists? I know I do. There's something God wants me to do or something I really should do, but instead of doing it, I run. I may not jump on a ship and sail across the ocean, but I'll jump on the Internet and sail through a few websites.

4. Why do you think we ignore the items on our to-do lists when we obviously want to do them since we were the ones who put them there?

Often my to-dos sound good when they're off in the distant future, but in the present they sound super boring or far too hard to tackle. I think I'll be happier if I ignore them, but I'm not. Instead, I wallow in the negative energy that comes from avoiding my list and suffer the consequences of ignoring it as well. I'm not the only one who has problems when I do what I feel like doing rather than what I should be doing.

5. Read Jonah 1:4–12. Did Jonah's do-what-you-want lifestyle make him happy? Explain.

Jonah had a valid reason for not wanting to help the Ninevites, but here's the interesting thing: Jonah did what he wanted, but it didn't make him happy. Instead we find him asleep on the boat, avoiding life and later telling the sailors to just throw him overboard.

6. We're not happy either when we procrastinate. Just think of your own life. How do you feel when you procrastinate day after day?

7. What kinds of activities do you do when you're procrastinating?

When I procrastinate writing, I don't sit down and have a quiet time or go outside for a refreshing walk or call a friend for coffee. Instead, I check my emails. I see if there are any new posts on Instagram. I think of random things to look up on the Internet. None of these activities are life-giving or loving. They're just draining time-wasters that I don't even enjoy all that much.

I'm far happier when I buckle down and finish my to-do list even when I don't feel like it—but I can't always make myself do that. Like Jonah, I need to see life from God's perspective if I want the strength to do the hard things on that list.

8. How do you think Jonah would have responded to God's request if he had taken the time to talk things over with God, forgiving the Ninevites for their past treatment of the Israelites, and maybe even praying for the Ninevites?

My guess is that Jonah would have actually wanted to obey God if he had taken the time to see the Ninevites through God's eyes. But without God's perspective, he just wanted to run. That's why it's so important to take the time to see life and work through God's eyes. Let's do that now with one of our own difficult tasks.

9. Can you think of anything God wants you to do—or anything *you* want yourself to do—that you've been avoiding? List that below.

10. What makes you not want to follow through on that?

11. Why do you think God wants you to work on that, or why do you want to work on it (at least in theory)?

12. What will happen if you do what you *feel* like doing rather than what God wants or what you want (at least in theory)?

13. What will be the ongoing consequences of your failure to act?

When I answered the last few questions, I actually wanted to do what God had called me to do, and I think I'll even follow through with that today when I finish editing this chapter. It helps to have God's perspective on individual to-dos, but it also helps to look at His will for our overall workday. We know He's called us to love others well (Matthew 22:36–40); let's see if that's happening in our day-to-day lives.

14. Think of all of the things you typically do (or want to do) in a day and list them below. Don't forget to add things like cooking dinner, watching TV, having your quiet time, and exercise. (We're trying to get a general idea of how we spend our time each day.)

15. Now go back and circle anything you listed that could be an act of love toward others if you went into it with the right attitude. What did you learn from this exercise?

Did you surprise yourself by how much of your to-do list is tied to loving others well? One thing you may want to check is to make sure all the activities you circled lie in the loving others category and not in the pleasing others or avoiding conflict or doing what's easy categories. Sometimes we do things we shouldn't do (such as chores our kids should be doing or saying yes to everyone who asks us to do something) just to avoid conflict or make people happy or because it's just plain easier that way.

16. Look over all the activities you listed in question 14. Do any of them fall into the "God would rather have me delegate or just say no" category? What would you gain by delegating or eliminating those things?

It's easy to talk about loving others well with our daily to-dos and embrace the *idea*, but it's incredibly hard to live it out on a daily basis. We can't do it without God's help. Remembering who we're loving by the various jobs on our lists and maybe even praying for those people while we work will help. Another habit that will help can be found in Philippians 4:8.

17. What does Paul tell us to do in that verse?

18. Let's see how this works with the to-do you mentioned in question 9. If you were to dwell on the "bad" in those to-dos, what kinds of things would you dwell on?

19. If you were to dwell on the "good" in those to-dos, what kinds of things would you dwell on? (Note: Sometimes the good in to-dos is the "future good"—how good you'll feel, how it will help others, or how it will change *your* life when it's done.)

20. How would your attitude toward your to-dos change if you were to dwell on the good?

If you have a tendency to dwell on the bad of your to-do list items like I do, try this: Put a little sticky note someplace where you'll see it each day that says, "Dwell on the good!" Then each day, before you start your next to-do, take a minute and dwell on the good of that to-do. Think about who you're loving, how it will change someone's life (maybe even yours), how good it will feel to get it done, and how good God is to give you the physical and mental capability to do it. Staying positive will help us follow through on our to-dos.

—◌ *Weekly Productivity Tips* ◌—

While it's true that we need to learn how to work even when we don't feel like it, it's also helpful to do what we can do to make work fun. Today's tips will give you some ideas for that.

1. **Try the Pomodoro method to get your work done.** With this method you work for 25-30 minutes, take a 5-minute break, then repeat as needed. The advantage is that you're training yourself to focus on work during that 25-30 minutes. It also helps to think of tasks in terms of how many pomodoros each task takes. For example, if I plan to write for two hours, I schedule four 30-minute pomodoros in my planner. For some reason, this seems less intimidating than scheduling two hours, especially when I know I can take breaks between my pomodoros. I use the Focus Time app from focustimeapp.com or a 30-minute OrgaNice Hourglass Sand Timer to time my work periods.

2. **Plan fun non-addictive activities for your breaks.** I'll often work on a puzzle for my five-minute breaks from writing. I use that time to either talk to God about my project or to stop thinking about the project altogether. A five-minute exercise break would be another good option.

3. **Work quickly.** When you have a job you don't want to do, try to do it as fast as you can, without thinking about it. That way you won't have time to dread it. (This tip is from one of my daughters; I just tried it yesterday and it worked!)

4. **Find ways to make the work itself fun.** For example, on days when I have lots of little jobs such as vacuuming or cleaning bathrooms, I'll write those jobs in my planner and number them. Then I'll put a bunch of numbers into a bowl and draw them out one at a time. If I draw the number '5,' for example, I'll look on my list to see which job is in the number 5 position and do that job. So even if the jobs themselves aren't fun, my process is fun, as it's always interesting to see what job I have to do next! I also use this process if I get behind on paperwork. I'll divide all the paperwork up into little piles (no more than five things in a pile), number the piles, and then draw numbers from the bowl to see which pile to work on. Between each pile of paperwork, I have the option of putting in five puzzle pieces if I want. Another way to make work fun is to play music or listen to a podcast while you're working.

Week Three

I CAN'T DO IT

I don't know how many times I've written "I can't do it" in my journal. If you've been working on overcoming procrastination for the last two weeks, my guess is that you've probably felt the same way: It's too hard. You can't do it. Or you can't even get yourself to *try* doing those hard jobs on your list.

Sure, we said we were going to renew our minds and work on our to-do lists each day, but let's face it: we're *procrastinators*. There's a good chance we haven't done what we said we would do!

Thankfully, God is here to help. He knows our weaknesses, and He knows we won't change overnight. But that doesn't mean He wants us to give up. No, He wants us to persevere! And that's what today's lesson is about: persevering even when it seems like there's no way we'll be able to do what God wants us to do. In today's lesson, we'll look at another person who didn't think he could do what God called him to do. Let's peek in on a conversation between God and Moses.

1. Read Exodus 3:1–10. What does God want Moses to do in Exodus 3:10?

2. Why did God want someone to bring the Israelites out of Egypt?

3. Moses knew what God wanted him to do because God was right there talking to him from a burning bush. Do you think we can assume God wants us to overcome procrastination? Why or why not? List as many reasons as possible.

4. I think it's safe to say God wants us to overcome procrastination, but He also knows it's hard to break free. Just think of your own journey these past couple of weeks. Has it been easy to make yourself renew your mind and work on those jobs you don't feel like doing? Describe the journey.

Sometimes we assume that if God wants us to do something He'll make it easy, but that's not true. Just think of Moses. God wanted him to lead the Israelites out of Egypt, but He didn't make it easy. Moses knew it would be hard, so he protested a bit before taking the job. Let's look at the reservations Moses had and see how God responded to him.

5. Read the passages on the following page, then record the conversation between God and Moses about why Moses didn't think he could do the job and God thought He *could* do it.

	What did Moses say to God?	What did God say (or give) to Moses?
Exodus 3:11-12		
Exodus 4:1-8		
Exodus 4:10-12		

Isn't that interesting? God doesn't just give Moses the promise of His presence and the right words to say. He also gives Moses a practical tool: a staff that turns into a snake and a hand that turns leprous on command. If God gave you something like that today, wouldn't you be a bit awestruck?

Moses, on the other hand, can't seem to get off his I-can't-do-this kick. As soon as God shows him the snake/leprous hand duo, Moses says, "But I don't speak well. I never have."

We do the same thing. God has blessed us with different abilities, strengths, spiritual gifts, life experiences, and education to do the things He's called us to do, but instead of focusing on those things and being thankful, we focus on our shortcomings: a list of reasons why we can't do what He has called us to do. Let's see what this looks like in our own lives.

6. What is something you're pretty sure God wants you to do, but you've been procrastinating it for weeks or months or maybe even years? (If you can't think of anything God has been wanting you to do, think of something *you've* been wanting you to do.)

7. Pretend God is talking to you right now. He's saying, "This week, I want you to do that thing you've been putting off forever." What reasons would you give Him for not being able to do that?

8. Review Exodus 3:12 and 4:11–12. How do you think God would respond to your protests?

9. Now review Exodus 4:1–8. Has God given you any natural strengths, character traits, spiritual gifts, or resources to help you do that project?

10. Remember Moses's reaction to the leprous hand and the staff/snake combo? Are you reacting like Moses and focusing more on your weaknesses (question 7) or on the ways God will or has already provided (questions 8-9)?

11. What would happen if you were to focus on God being with you to help you and all the things He's *already* given you to help with this project?

12. It's also important to think about getting outside help for our projects. What did God give Moses in Exodus 4:13–16 to help him with his project besides the staff and a promise to put words in his mouth?

Isn't that interesting? God could have just said, "Moses, I *told* you I would give you the words to speak. Don't worry about it," but He didn't. Instead, He gave Moses a helper: Aaron. Sometimes we need helpers with our projects as well. That helper could be a friend, family member, employee, book, online support group, coach, accountability partner, or even Google. I don't know how many times I've googled things like "how to start a podcast" when I've been stuck on a work project. It's far easier to learn how to do a project from an expert than to muddle through on my own.

13. Think of the project you mentioned in question 6. Do you think you need help with that project? If so, who or what do you think could help you with your project? Review the last paragraph if you need ideas.

It helps to know God will equip us to do what He wants us to do and that we can also get outside help. But if we want to persevere without getting discouraged, we'll also need to have realistic expectations for our projects.

14. Think of everything you know about the Israelites' journey from the time God called Moses to the day they entered the Promised Land. Do you think Moses ever got discouraged or wondered if they would ever make it to the Promised Land? If so, why do you think he persevered when it was so hard?

15. Now think of your own journey to overcome procrastination and also the project you mentioned in question 6. Do you think God will make it easy for you or do you think there will be some failures, disappointments, and hardships along the way? Explain.

The truth is, there *will* be struggles along the way. That's why it's so important to develop a renewing-the-mind habit—so we can see our projects, goals, and even our quest to overcome procrastination from a biblical perspective. Moses spent lots of time with God, and he needed that time with God to keep going.

Some of his time with God involved questions (Exodus 5:22–23), but other times were transcendent (Exodus 34:29). When struggles come, our temptation is to go to the refrigerator or Netflix or social media for escape. Moses didn't have those options. He went to God.

16. What do you think would happen if you went to God whenever you were tempted to give up on your projects and took the time to renew your mind and discuss your projects with Him?

Often we think of weakness and failure and suffering as bad things, but God doesn't see it that way. Not only does He use trials to mature us (Romans 5:3–5), He often chooses weak people to do His work, fully knowing He's taking them out of their comfort zones, so of course they're going to suffer.

Moses is an example. You would think if God wanted someone to talk the Pharaoh into letting the Israelites leave Egypt, He would have chosen a salesman-type of person: a charismatic leader with a gift for words. But God didn't. He chose Moses: a non-charismatic non-leader who wasn't good at speaking.

17. Why do you think God chose Moses to lead the children out of Egypt?

Here's what I've noticed in the Bible. God takes incompetent, ill-equipped-for-the-job people and then He equips them to do His work. Because they're ill-equipped, they're forced to rely on God. He uses that reliance to grow their character and draw them near to Him. The problem is that we don't always draw near to Him. Jonah is an example.

18. Review Jonah 1:3 and Exodus 3:1–4:12. Neither Jonah nor Moses wanted to do what God asked them to do. What was different about how they responded to their unwanted jobs from God?

Moses chose to visit with God about his misgivings and fears, and God was able to show him a biblical perspective—namely that God would equip him and help him. Jonah didn't discuss his misgivings with God; he just ran, missing out on the biblical perspective that would have helped him follow through on the dreaded task.

When we take the time to renew our minds when we feel like procrastinating, we're being like Moses—talking to God about our fears and misgivings and the reasons we're dreading the task. This gives God an opportunity to talk to us about how He'll equip us and why He wants us to do something. My prayer is that you'll have the strength to go to God this week to renew your mind when you don't feel like working on your to-do list.

19. If you haven't been able to make yourself do that yet, can you think of anything you could do to make it more likely you'll be able to renew your mind each day?

If God could equip Moses to lead the Israelites out of Egypt, He can certainly equip us for our daily to-dos! It's exciting to think about what God will do in our lives—both in regard to what we can accomplish when we develop a daily to-do-list habit and also in regard to how He'll mature us as we persevere with our to-do lists even when they're super hard. Try to follow through with your to-do lists once again for 5-6 days this week and renew your mind each day before you work on it. Let's get started with this week's project.

—⌁ *Procrastination Project* ⌁—

You have two options for your to-do lists this week: 1) you can continue on like you've been doing the first two weeks, listing your top three tasks each day and working on those, or 2) you can choose to keep doing what you've been doing but also add a task or two each day from a bigger project. Before you decide, let's brainstorm a bit.

20. Can you think of any projects you haven't done because you don't know how to do them or because they're too hard or too big? List those below. (Don't forget to include the project you listed in question 6, if appropriate.)

21. Would you like to add one of these projects to your to-do list each day? If so, which project would you like to work on? (Note: If you're just barely getting by, it might be more helpful to hold off on any big

projects until you're more consistent with completing your to-do list each day—but do whatever you think best.)

If you decide to work on a big project, read the productivity tips below, then break your project into easily manageable tasks. If you decide to continue what you've been doing, read the tips anyway as they'll be helpful even for smaller projects.

—ↄ Weekly Productivity Tips ↄ—

1. **Research how to do the project.** Often projects and goals seem overwhelming because we don't know how to do them. We'll save time in the long run if we do a little research and find the easiest way possible to do the project—just don't spend too much time on your research as that can also become a procrastination technique!

2. **Break large—and even small—projects into small manageable tasks.** Since we don't usually procrastinate things that are fun and easy, it's helpful to break large projects into small tasks that are relatively easy to complete. For example, if my project is to lead a Bible study at church and I've never done that before, I might procrastinate it forever because it's so overwhelming. If I take the time to break the project into steps though, all of a sudden it seems more manageable.

   Here are some steps I might list for that project: 1) Google "how to lead a Bible study at my church," 2) ask friends for Bible study suggestions, 3) search for a good Bible study online, 4) choose a Bible study, 5) decide when to start and how many weeks it will be, 6) write an announcement, 7) give announcement to church secretary, 8) get the leaders guide if there is one, 9) read leaders guide, 10) make an overall plan for the study, and 11) plan the first day.

When I transfer these tasks to my daily to-do list, I won't put "work on Bible study" on my list. Instead, I'll put "Google how to lead a Bible study" on my list. If I wanted to do a couple of tasks each day, I might put "Do steps 1 and 2" on my list as a single task. I would only do that, though, if the combination of those tasks were fairly easy, non-intimidating, and didn't take too much time.

3. **Problem solve if you have a glitch.** Often, we'll be sailing along with a project when all of a sudden, we come up against a wall. When that happens, try asking the following questions: 1) What's the problem? 2) Why is that a problem? 3) What are some possible solutions? 4) Are you believing any lies? 5) What is the truth to each lie? 6) What's the best solution, recognizing that there's (almost) never a perfect solution? (Note: You can download these questions in a problem-solving worksheet at barbraveling.com/procrastination.)

If you've decided to take on a more difficult project this week, go to page 157 and use one of the project lists to plan steps for your project, estimating the amount of time each step will take. If your project has more than ten steps, write the first ten steps on the project list and then plan more when you're finished with those. Don't forget to add "research how to do this project" if you don't know how to do it.

For small and medium-sized projects, each of these steps should be a task you can add to your daily to-do list. For larger projects like writing books, you may have more time-consuming tasks such as brainstorm ideas for the book, write an outline, write first draft, etc. A couple of those tasks could take hours, so when you get to that task on your schedule, you may have to make another project list to break down that task into actionable steps. You could also just put something like "write one hour" on your list if that works better for you.

Week Four

I'M TOO OVERWHELMED TO DO IT

It's Saturday morning at 9:00 and I'm sitting at my computer trying to write this week's study. I'm teaching it on Tuesday to a group of ladies from my church, and all I have ready so far is an outline. The reason I have so little written is because I'm completely overwhelmed with life at the moment—too many projects and I can't keep track of them.

You might think I'd be up working from sunup to sundown to get everything done, but I'm not. Instead, I usually get up, do two or three hours of work, start thinking about everything else I need to do, then spend the rest of the day wasting time because I know I'll never be able to get it all done.

Can you relate? Do you ever have days where you're so overwhelmed with life and work that you can't get yourself to do anything? Or are you the type of person who works too much when life gets busy? Both responses can take us away from our main goal of loving God and others well. Today we'll look at three people in the Bible who had too much on their plates and see how they handled it: Moses, Martha, and Jesus. Let's begin with Moses and Martha.

1. Read the following Bible passages and list the circumstances that were making Moses and Martha feel as though they couldn't do it all.

	What circumstances were causing this person to feel overwhelmed?
Moses: Exodus 18:5-18	
Martha: Luke 10:38-40	

Martha reminds me of the 23-year-old-newlywed me. The first few times my hubby and I had guests for dinner, I made the preparations far more complicated than they needed to be. I'd rush around cleaning our two-room (no bedroom) apartment, making everything from scratch, and was always completely stressed by the time the guests arrived.

2. If you were to give advice to me back in those days, what would you have told me?

I'm hoping you would have told me to stop feeling like everything had to be so perfect and just focus on my guests! We can't know for sure because we don't know Martha, but I suspect she was stressed because she was making dinner far more complicated than it needed to be. Most of us have at least one area of our lives that could be enhanced by relaxing our standards and settling for "good enough." For me, it's decision making. I make decisions far more complicated than they need to be because I want the "perfect" decision (which doesn't normally exist). I used to be like that with writing, too, but I realized as I was editing this study that God has changed me in this area. I now enjoy writing, in large part because I'm no longer a perfectionist in this area.

3. Can you think of any areas of your own life that would be enhanced by relaxing your standards and settling for "good enough"? Here are some examples: exercise, cleaning, studying, decision making, cooking, appearance, homeschooling, planning vacations, or work-related projects.

Sometimes we're stressed because we're making our standards too high, but other times we're overwhelmed because we just plain have too much to do. Moses fell into this category.

4. Why do you think Moses didn't get someone to help him with the disputes?

Sometimes I wonder if Moses was just blindly doing what everyone asked him to do without even thinking about it. I can relate. When I was younger, I didn't even consider "no" as an option. I just did what everyone asked me to do. This only works if people are asking us to do the things God wants us to do, but often they're asking us to do far more than is good for us. Just think of your own life.

5. Is there anything you're doing just because others are expecting you to do it, or because you feel like you *should* do it? Explain.

6. In Exodus 18:18, Jethro tells Moses, "It's not good what you're doing." So even though Moses was loving people well through ministry, Jethro told him it wasn't good because Moses was doing too much. Think of your own life. Do you have a "good" amount of work, or are you doing too much? Explain.

Often we end up in the "too much" category because we have unrealistic expectations for what we can accomplish. If you're constantly feeling overwhelmed with life, there's a good chance you have unrealistic expectations for yourself. This can be hard to see because we just charge through life thinking we can do it all. Let's take a minute to see if that's true.

7. If you feel like you're doing too much, list the projects, chores, responsibilities, or social obligations that add stress to your life. Be specific. If you don't feel like you're doing too much, list the things you do too perfectly or the things you regularly procrastinate (including decisions) because those are the things that can make you feel overwhelmed.

When I answered this question early in the writing of this book, I couldn't believe the number of things I was procrastinating. No wonder I was feeling stressed. I went from thinking I had a "good" amount of work (if only I could manage it better) to realizing I had way too much work and needed to start eliminating some things.

I worked on that throughout the course of this book and when I answered the question just now during the last edit of the book, I realized how much progress I've made. It's important to examine our lives and see if we're trying to do too much because there are consequences to living in a constant state of having too much to do. We see that in the life of Martha and Moses.

8. Read the Bible passages below to see how Martha and Moses were being affected by their long list of things to do.

	What were the consequences of having too much to do on both a practical and emotional level?
Moses: Exodus 18:18	
Martha: Luke 10:40-41	

9. Having too much to do wasn't working for Moses and Martha, and it doesn't work for us either. Just think of your own life. How does having too much on your schedule (or to-do list) negatively affect your life on both a practical and emotional level?

It's interesting to note that Jesus didn't solve Martha's problem by telling Mary to help. He knew that what Martha really needed was to sit down and spend some time with Him. We need that too. When we're busy, it's more important than ever to spend time with God so He can strengthen us and speak truth to us, reminding us of what's important in life.

One of the biggest dangers of being too busy is the effect it can have on our relationship with God if we skip time with Him each day to get our work done. It was obviously having that effect on Martha, but it was also causing problems in Martha's relationship with her sister Mary.

Having too much to do affects relationships in several different ways: First, it can make us grumpy and not fun to be around. Second, it keeps us from spending time with our loved ones. Third, it can cause us to neglect household responsibilities which often causes tension in relationships. Fourth, it can make us annoyed with people if we're busy and they're just sitting there. And finally, it can make us annoyed with others if the reason we're busy is because we're living up to their expectations. That's another situation where we need to visit with God to see if He wants us to do what others are expecting us to do.

10. If you're feeling overwhelmed right now, is it negatively affecting any of the people in your life or hurting any of your relationships, including your relationship with God? Explain.

11. Thankfully, we don't need to stay overwhelmed. Let's go back to Scripture again to look for solutions. Read the following passages and fill out the chart below.

	What was the solution for having too much to do?
Moses: Exodus 18:19-24	
Martha: Luke 10:42	
Jesus: Luke 5:15-16	

Isn't that interesting? The Bible gives us both practical and spiritual solutions for busyness: get others to help you with your work (Moses), simplify (Martha), don't do things just because people expect you to do them (Jesus), and spend more time with God (Martha and Jesus). This last bit of advice seems hard to understand. How can spending time with God make us more productive? Wouldn't it be better to just get to work? Jesus answers these questions by the example He set for us.

12. Why do you think Jesus spent so much time going off to pray when there were thousands of people wanting to visit with Him and be healed by Him?

When I'm overwhelmed I either a) get paralyzed and completely avoid my to-do list, b) get obsessed and work in a frenzy, or c) get smart and work in an orderly fashion, taking frequent breaks to talk to God throughout the day so I don't get stressed. I can tell you from experience that option "c" is by far the best option. Not only do I get more done, but I live in peace because God keeps me peaceful in the midst of turmoil.

During my breaks with God, I often work through a set of questions from *The Renewing of the Mind Project*. Other times I'll go for a walk and talk with God or sit down and do a puzzle while talking to Him. Sometimes I just stop writing and spend a few minutes talking to Him right there at my desk. These times with God almost always leave me refreshed and ready to get back to work with a much clearer mind than before. The only time they don't is when I'm in such a frenzy that I can't focus on God. It's far better to renew our minds *before* we get in a frenzy than afterward!

If you work full-time, try to squeeze in time during the day to renew your mind if you find yourself getting stressed about work. I've had coaching clients tell me they take a break at work to walk the halls, jump on the company treadmill, or go to the lunchroom to renew their minds by meditating on Scripture or running through a set of questions from my *I Deserve a Donut* app. It may only be a three-minute break, but it will greatly help your attitude throughout the day.

If you're home with little kids, you'll have to get creative to find "alone" time. When our kids were little, they did a lot of playing with each other so it would have been pretty easy for me to pull out my journal and renew my mind while I was watching the kids or pray while I was cleaning or cooking. Also, don't forget to have realistic expectations about how much you can accomplish if you're caring for young children, working a 40-hour week, or have health issues that deplete your energy.

Another thing that will help us avoid a frenzy is to spend some time working on reducing the "too much to do" in our lives. This can be done both by overcoming procrastination and also by making a deliberate effort to see what needs to change so we can live a less overwhelmed life.

It's easy to see what needs to change in the lives of Martha and Moses, but it's not always easy to see what needs to change in our own lives because everything seems so routine to us. We don't question why we do what we do. Sometimes it helps to take a step back and look at our lives from an outside perspective. Let's see if we can do that.

13. Pretend you're a stranger reading about your life in a book (review questions 5-7 to see the book). What advice would you give yourself as to why you're overwhelmed and how to get over it? (Brainstorm as many ideas as possible. Just because you write it down, it doesn't mean you need to do it.)

Often we're stressed because we have too much to do, but sometimes we're stressed because we're going through a difficult trial. When we're emotionally distraught, it's hard to make ourselves work. When that happens to me, I try to take time to visit with God and renew my mind about the trial first and then tackle my to-do list. Often I use the emotions questions from the *Renewing of the Mind Project* to help me with that. But if it's a really difficult trial, I give myself grace and try not to schedule too much.

If I'm stressed because of too much work, I sometimes go through the beginning-of-the-day stress questions in my *I Deserve a Donut* app as they help me prioritize and focus (although since writing this book, I don't do that as much as I now have the habit of focusing on the three most important things to do each day). But some days I just waste the whole day away and feel super depressed.

As you work on overcoming procrastination, try to remember that it's a process. You'll have good days and bad days. Don't get discouraged on the bad days; just know that a good day is coming. God will help you overcome procrastination, but He probably won't do it all in one day. If He does, write and tell me about it because I always like to hear about miracles. If He hasn't done that yet, let's get started on this week's project.

This week you have one of four options for your procrastination project: 1) continue to list your three most important tasks for the day and work on those, 2) continue to work on your big project from last week's study in combination with regular life jobs, 3) do an "elimination" project in combination with regular jobs, or 4) work on a "delegation" project in combination with regular jobs. Let's look at the last two options more closely.

—ᕙ Delegation Project ᕘ—

One of the ways to make life less overwhelming is to delegate some of your work. If you have kids at home, you could start a chore system where the kids do the work. If you have a home business, you could hire someone to do some of your business tasks. If you have the resources available, you could also hire someone to do things like yard work or housework. One of the things that keeps us from delegating is that it's hard work to set it up. In fact, the set-up itself is a project. Review the productivity tips in Week 3, then break your delegation project into steps, and work on it throughout the week.

—ᕙ Elimination Project ᕘ—

For an elimination project, you would look at what you wrote in questions 5–7 and 13, then spend some time in prayer and thought to see if you need to change anything about the way you do life. The time spent in prayer and thought is part of the project because it takes time to think through life and make a change. Plan to spend 15-30 minutes a day on this project, or plan a one to two-hour block of time to preferably get out of the house and think and pray through everything. Once you decide what to eliminate, spend the rest of the week working on implementing those changes.

Here are some examples of things you might decide to eliminate or simplify: get rid of a social media account, set up one or two nights a week with no social obligations (this is especially important if you're an introvert), remove yourself from an optional leadership position, give yourself a time limit on how long you can spend on something you typically spend way too much time on, set up a rotating menu plan for evening meals, or plan to purposely procrastinate some project (for example, I have a cupboard full of old photographs I'm not planning to even think about until I'm 80—because I've set that boundary, the photos don't stress me out). If you choose a complicated project, such as setting up a rotating menu plan (this eliminates decision making each day about what to have for dinner), then write down the steps you'll need to take to make it happen.

—❧ *Procrastination Project* ❧—

Go ahead and choose your project but try not to spend too much time on the decision. If nothing is coming to mind or if you feel like it would be better to keep working on your daily list or big project, continue to do what you did last week. Record your commitment below.

14. This week I will try to accomplish the following with God's help:

—❧ *Weekly Productivity Tips* ❧—

1. **Do the worst first.** Often, we're overwhelmed because we're putting off a difficult job or decision. If you do that job first thing in the morning, you'll feel better right away because you won't have all of that negative energy eating away at you all day. Don't forget to renew your mind if you can't make yourself do it.

2. Have a weekly and/or daily theme. I used to work on several different projects each day without finishing any of them. I've discovered I'm much more relaxed if I see one project through to completion rather than having several projects going at once. I'll actually plan a theme for the week and then assign tasks for that focus each day. If I look in my current planner, I have one week dedicated to working on this Bible study, another week for podcasts, another week for setting up my coaching practice, and another week for working on book translations. I won't finish most of those projects in a week's time, but it will still help me be less overwhelmed to just have one focus for the week. If you don't have any big projects going, consider having a different theme for each day of the week.

3. Let go of perfectionism, being all things to all people, and doing everything yourself. Yes, I know, this is easier said than done. But if we don't let go of those things, we'll continue to be overwhelmed with life—because here's the truth, friends: We will never be perfect, we will disappoint people, and if we keep trying to do everything ourselves, we will go crazy! That said, learning to change in these areas is a process. It will take both practical changes and lots of renewing and going to God for help to get ourselves to change in these areas.

4. Do an end-of-day work detox. Often we'll get to the end of the day and either wonder what we did all day or feel stressed because we didn't finish our to-do list for the day. One thing that's really helped me with this is to do an end-of-day detox. At the end of most workdays, I'll sit down and go through a set of questions and visit with God about the day. This helps me to mentally put the workday aside and move on to dinner and an evening without work. I've included the questions on the following page and also in the Daily Renewing Activities section of this book in case you'd like to give them a try.

—ᴄᴏ *Barb's End-of-Day Work Detox Questions* ᴏᴄ—

1. What did you get done today?

2. What did you do well today?

3. What could you have done better today?

4. What do you need to remember to do tomorrow? (Do you want to make a list for tomorrow?)

5. Are you believing any lies? If so, what's the truth to each lie?

6. What will you need to accept to stop thinking about work tonight?

7. Do you think God wants you to accept that? Why or why not?

8. What will you do for refreshment and nourishment tonight?

9. What will you do with your computer and phone so you can have fun? (I ask this question to remind myself to put them both away so I don't waste time on them in the evening!)

Week Five

I'M TOO AFRAID TO DO IT

When I began writing my current blog back in 2013, I would sometimes wake up in the middle of the night in a cold sweat and run upstairs to change my blog post that was supposed to go out that morning. I was terrified the post wouldn't be good enough and that people would condemn me. This fear often made me procrastinate the writing of my posts.

Sometimes our projects, goals, and to-dos are comfortable—things like planting a garden—but other times they're downright scary. Maybe we've failed at these goals before and are afraid to try again. Or maybe we're afraid people will condemn us for the way we do our to-dos. Or maybe we're afraid to put in a huge amount of effort or money when we don't know if the projects will be successful or not.

Whatever the reason, these fears can paralyze us and keep us from moving ahead with our work. In today's Bible study, we'll look at two different groups of people from the Bible who found themselves in scary situations: our old friends the Israelites who now find themselves on the brink of entering the Promised Land and three new characters: Shadrach, Meshach, and Abednego. Let's see how they responded when faced with some scary situations.

1. Read the Bible passages and fill in the chart on the following page.

	Israelites Numbers 13:1–14:4	Shadrach, Meshach, and Abednego Daniel 3:1–18
What was the scary situation?		
What was the possible negative outcome?		
How did they respond to their scary situation?		
What did they focus on in the midst of their scary situation?		

2. What did you learn from these examples about the best way to handle scary situations?

One thing I learned is that I need to focus on God, not the giants. The Israelites focused on the giants and ended up wandering in the desert for forty years (Numbers 14). We do the same thing. We focus on all the things that could go wrong with our projects (or are already going wrong) and end up wandering in the desert of procrastination for years because we're too afraid of what will happen if we move forward. Let's see what this looks like on a personal level.

3. Can you think of any area of your life (a decision, scary goal, or a big project, for example) where you're wandering in the desert because you're afraid of what will happen if you move ahead? Explain. (Note: If you can't think of anything, just list the to-do that you're most dreading.)

4. What is the possible negative outcome with this decision, goal, or project if you follow through with your plan?

5. Often we don't follow through on plans because we're too focused on the "giants" in the situation. Are you more focused on God or the giants in this situation? If it's the giants, how is that affecting your attitude and your progress with the project?

6. What would happen if you were to focus more on God than the giants?

It's easy to see the bad things that could happen if we follow through on our plans and decisions, but we don't always see the bad things that will happen if we keep putting off those plans and decisions. If we want to break free from procrastination, we need to see how it affects us.

7. What will happen if you procrastinate the project or decision you mentioned in question 3 indefinitely?

Sometimes we don't move ahead with scary decisions and projects for legitimate reasons. But other times we really should move ahead—we're just too scared to do it. This happened to me when I wrote my first book, *Freedom from Emotional Eating*. I wanted to help people, but I also didn't want to write a book that no one would read.

I spent months praying and asking God if He wanted me to write the book. I thought I just wanted to know His will, but later I realized what I really wanted was an assurance that people would read it if I went through the trouble to write it. God never gave me that assurance, but I wrote the book anyway. I felt like it was the least I could do for a God who had done so much for me.

In talking to others, I've found that I'm not alone in this. Often we procrastinate because we don't know whether or not God wants us to do something, but what we really want is the assurance that things will turn out okay if we move ahead with our plans.

8. Are you currently procrastinating a decision or project because you don't know what God's will is or because you don't know how it will turn out? If so, what's your worst fear with that project or decision?

9. What is making you want to say "yes" to this project or decision?

10. Do you think it's possible you're doing the same thing I did with my first book—waiting for a sign from God that everything will go smoothly if you go ahead with your plan? If so, what would you gain by making the decision and either moving ahead with the project or saying no to it, trusting that God will take care of you even if things don't go well or even if people get mad at you?

I'm all about praying over decisions, looking at biblical mandates and principles that come into play, considering the practical pros and cons, and getting advice—but at some point we just need to make the decision. Choosing to *not* make a decision is actually a decision in and of itself. It's a decision to live in indecision which is a terrible place to live. Interestingly, God gave the Israelites the assurance they would be victorious in conquering the Promised Land, but he didn't assure Shadrach, Meshach, and Abednego that He would protect them from the fire.

11. Read Daniel 3:17–18. What was the attitude of Shadrach, Meshach, and Abednego in regard to moving ahead with their plan even though they didn't have the assurance that God would make everything go well?

12. What I love about Shadrach, Meshach, and Abednego is that they believed God would save them from the fiery furnace, but they also recognized He might not—but either way, they were going to worship Him. Let's see what this would look like in our own lives. What would it look like to have Shadrach, Meshach, and Abednego's attitude in the situation you mentioned in questions 8-10?

If we can keep clearly in our minds that God is enough, we'll be much more likely to have a good attitude and not be fearful, because here's the truth: Often our fears *do* come true! God made it easy for Shadrach, Meshach, and Abednego, but He doesn't make it easy for everyone. Moses is an example.

13. Let's look at some of the fears Moses may have had in Egypt and see if those fears came true. I'll list the fears on the left. Look up the passages on the right to see if they came true.

Moses's Potential Fears	According to the following Bible verses, did Moses's potential fears come true?
That the Israelites wouldn't listen to him	Exodus 6:9 (read Exodus 6:2–8 for context):
That he'd be condemned by others and not live up to their expectations	Exodus 5:20–21 (read Exodus 5:1–19 for context):
Fear of failure	Exodus 5:22–23, 7:22, 8:15, 8:19, etc.:
That it would be super hard and not very fun	Exodus 11:10-15:
That he wouldn't be rewarded for his efforts	Numbers 20:12 (read Numbers 20:1–11 for context):

Isn't that interesting? All of Moses's potential fears came true, yet he didn't give up. Yes, he got discouraged. Yes, he doubted God. Yes, he had his little temper tantrums. And yes, he was insecure and fearful. But through it all, he remained faithful to God by not giving up. Moses persevered through countless trials and earned his way into the Hebrews Hall of Fame for his faith (Hebrews 11:24–28), yet when we first see Moses talking to God in the burning bush, he had very little faith. God changed Moses and helped him grow through the process of following Him even when life was hard. God can also help us grow when we persevere with our scary projects and decisions.

14. Read James 1:2–4 and think of your own decision or project. Can you think of any ways God could use that project or decision to help you mature if you follow through with it?

God will help us mature if we persevere with our projects and decisions. He'll also help us grow in the fruit of self-control in regard to the way we use our time (Galatians 5:22–23). If you think of fruit on a tree, it doesn't come all at once in one glorious harvest. Instead, each year the tree produces fruit. That's how it will be with our growth in overcoming procrastination. Each year we'll get a little better if we keep going to God for the sustenance we need to grow and bear fruit.

As you continue to work on overcoming procrastination, try to remember it's a step-by-step process. Just as the Israelites weren't delivered from Egypt overnight, you won't be delivered from procrastination overnight.

My prayer for both of us as we finish this study is that we'll be like Moses and persevere even when life gets hard and our projects aren't turning out the way we want them to. Let's work together on one last project.

—✄ *Procrastination Project* ✄—

This week you have two choices. Either you can continue with a project from a previous week, or you can try a new project that takes you out of your comfort zone. It might be a goal you'd like to pursue, a decision you need to make, or even a business or ministry you'd like to start. Think of different ideas you've had that you've discarded, thinking, *No, I'd never be able to do that.* If you choose to work on a goal or a business/ministry idea, read the first tip in the Weekly Productivity Tip section and give that project a whirl with the idea that you'll just try working on it for a couple of hours and see how it goes with no commitment to continue after this week. Let's take a minute to brainstorm possible projects.

15. List a few decisions you need to make or projects you've considered doing that scare you or take you out of your comfort zone. If you can't think of any big projects (or don't have time for big projects at this stage of your life), think of small scary projects such as "find a new dentist" or "ask a new friend to lunch" or "introduce yourself to someone at church and have a conversation with them."

16. Go ahead and choose one of the above projects or decisions to work on, a project from a previous week, or a to-do list strategy like we did the first two weeks. Record your commitment below. (Note: If you decide to work on a decision project and are having a difficult time making a decision, try renewing your mind with the "I Don't Know What to Do So I'll Do Nothing" renewing activity on page 134.)

—◦ *Weekly Productivity Tips* ◦—

1. **Have a "this is just an experiment" attitude.** Too often we're fearful because we feel like everything needs to be perfect. One way to avoid this mentality is to think of what we're doing as an experiment: We'll just give it a whirl and see how it goes.

2. **Connect with others who are working on the same types of projects.** Sometimes it helps to have a listening ear. When we realize others are struggling with the same issues we're experiencing, it eases our fears.

3. **Hold "success" with open hands.** If we want to let go of our fears, we need to let go of the need to be liked, respected, successful, and rewarded for our efforts. The more we hold the outcome with open hands, the less fearful we'll be. It's far easier to hold the outcome with open hands when we remember that life is about God and that He is enough. So my best practical tip for this section is to renew your mind every time your fears come up so you remember God is enough, even if your plans don't turn out the way you want.

DAILY TO-DO LISTS AND ACCOUNTABILITY CHARTS

Day	Did you make your list?	Was your list realistic based on time estimates?	Did you renew?	How many tasks can you celebrate completing today?

Check out the "Sample To-Do List and Accountability Chart" on page 154 if you need help with this section.

What did you learn this week?

What are the three most important things you'd like to accomplish today? List them below.

✓	Day: Theme:	Time Estimate	D or I	Priority

What are the three most important things you'd like to accomplish today? List them below.

✓	Day: Theme:	Time Estimate	D or I	Priority

What are the three most important things you'd like to accomplish today? List them below.

✓	Day: Theme:	Time Estimate	D or I	Priority

What are the three most important things you'd like to accomplish today? List them below.

✓	Day: Theme:	Time Estimate	D or I	Priority

What are the three most important things you'd like to accomplish today? List them below.

✓	Day: Theme:	Time Estimate	D or I	Priority

What are the three most important things you'd like to accomplish today? List them below.

✓	Day: Theme:	Time Estimate	D or I	Priority

— ↶ *Week Two* ↷ —

Day	Did you make your list?	Was your list realistic based on time estimates?	Did you renew?	How many tasks can you celebrate completing today?

What did you learn this week?

What are the three most important things you'd like to accomplish today? List them below.

✓	Day:	Theme:	Time Estimate	D or I	Priority

What are the three most important things you'd like to accomplish today? List them below.

✓	Day:	Theme:	Time Estimate	D or I	Priority

What are the three most important things you'd like to accomplish today? List them below.

✓	Day:	Theme:	Time Estimate	D or I	Priority

What are the three most important things you'd like to accomplish today? List them below.

✓	Day:	Theme:	Time Estimate	D or I	Priority

What are the three most important things you'd like to accomplish today? List them below.

✓	Day:	Theme:	Time Estimate	D or I	Priority

What are the three most important things you'd like to accomplish today? List them below.

✓	Day:	Theme:	Time Estimate	D or I	Priority

─◌ *Week Three* ◌─

Day	Did you make your list?	Was your list realistic based on time estimates?	Did you renew?	How many tasks can you celebrate completing today?

What did you learn this week?

What are the three most important things you'd like to accomplish today? List them below.

✓	Day: Theme:	Time Estimate	D or I	Priority

What are the three most important things you'd like to accomplish today? List them below.

✓	Day: Theme:	Time Estimate	D or I	Priority

What are the three most important things you'd like to accomplish today? List them below.

✓	Day:	Theme:	Time Estimate	D or I	Priority

What are the three most important things you'd like to accomplish today? List them below.

✓	Day:	Theme:	Time Estimate	D or I	Priority

What are the three most important things you'd like to accomplish today? List them below.

✓	Day:	Theme:	Time Estimate	D or I	Priority

What are the three most important things you'd like to accomplish today? List them below.

✓	Day:	Theme:	Time Estimate	D or I	Priority

❧ Week Four ❧

Day	Did you make your list?	Was your list realistic based on time estimates?	Did you renew?	How many tasks can you celebrate completing today?

What did you learn this week?

What are the three most important things you'd like to accomplish today? List them below.

✓	Day:　　　　　Theme:	Time Estimate	D or I	Priority

What are the three most important things you'd like to accomplish today? List them below.

✓	Day:　　　　　Theme:	Time Estimate	D or I	Priority

What are the three most important things you'd like to accomplish today? List them below.

✓	Day: Theme:	Time Estimate	D or I	Priority

What are the three most important things you'd like to accomplish today? List them below.

✓	Day: Theme:	Time Estimate	D or I	Priority

What are the three most important things you'd like to accomplish today? List them below.

✓	Day: Theme:	Time Estimate	D or I	Priority

What are the three most important things you'd like to accomplish today? List them below.

✓	Day: Theme:	Time Estimate	D or I	Priority

❧ Week Five ❧

Day	Did you make your list?	Was your list realistic based on time estimates?	Did you renew?	How many tasks can you celebrate completing today?

What did you learn this week?

What are the three most important things you'd like to accomplish today? List them below.

✓	Day:	Theme:	Time Estimate	D or I	Priority

What are the three most important things you'd like to accomplish today? List them below.

✓	Day:	Theme:	Time Estimate	D or I	Priority

What are the three most important things you'd like to accomplish today? List them below.

✓	Day: Theme:	Time Estimate	D or I	Priority

What are the three most important things you'd like to accomplish today? List them below.

✓	Day: Theme:	Time Estimate	D or I	Priority

What are the three most important things you'd like to accomplish today? List them below.

✓	Day: Theme:	Time Estimate	D or I	Priority

What are the three most important things you'd like to accomplish today? List them below.

✓	Day: Theme:	Time Estimate	D or I	Priority

DAILY RENEWING ACTIVITIES

When you feel like procrastinating, choose a renewing activity based on your reason for not wanting to do the next thing on your list.

IT'S NOT THAT BIG OF A DEAL IF I SKIP IT TODAY.

For God has not given us a spirit of timidity, but of power and love and discipline.
2 TIMOTHY 1:7

How does this passage apply to your current to-do?

LACK OF IMPORTANCE QUESTIONS

1. Why do you feel like it's not a big deal if you don't work on your project (or habit) today?

2. If you decide to take the day off, will you be more inclined to take the day off tomorrow as well? Why or why not?

3. Why do you want to develop this habit or accomplish this goal?

4. Do you think God wants you to develop this habit or accomplish this goal? Why or why not?

    a. Yes: If so, what will you need to sacrifice to do what He wants you to do?

    b. No: If not, what's driving you to work on this project? What would you have to sacrifice to give up this project?

    c. God doesn't care: Why would you like to finish this project or accomplish this goal? What will you need to sacrifice to accomplish your goal?

4. Is starting this habit (or achieving this goal) worth the sacrifice? Why or why not?

5. Is it worth the sacrifice even on days you don't feel like working on it?

6. What will happen if you're not willing to make that sacrifice?

7. Do you want that to happen?

8. If you want to develop this habit (or reach this goal), will you eventually have to make the sacrifice to work on it?

9. If so, what would be the advantage of getting started right now?

10. What do you think God wants to teach you through this trial?

11. What can you thank Him for?

I'M TOO BUSY. I DON'T HAVE TIME TO WORK ON THIS.

So teach us to number our days, that we may present to You a heart of wisdom.

PSALM 90:12

How does this passage apply to your current to-do?

LACK OF TIME OR PERFECT CONDITIONS QUESTIONS

1. Why do you feel like you can't work on your goal or to-do list today?

2. How much time would it take to do it?

3. Which of the following is true:

   a. You really don't have time to work on it.

   b. You could make the time, but you'd rather not. *

   c. You dread the thought of working on your goal or to-do list, and time is a good excuse. *

   d. You feel like you need the perfect conditions to work on it and conditions aren't ideal right now.

4. Is life always perfect, or do you sometimes have to make do and adjust your plans?

5. Is this one of those days where you'll have to adjust your plans if you want to accomplish your goal? Explain.

6. Think of the day ahead. When can you fit in time to work on your goal or to-do list?

7. Would you like to make a new plan to do that? If so, what is your plan?

8. What will happen if you consistently put off this project when conditions aren't perfect?

9. What would be the value of working on it today even though conditions aren't perfect?

10. Is there anything you need to accept?

*If this is true, determine the real reason you don't want to work on your project and use one of the other sets of questions to renew your mind.

BUT THERE'S A GOOD REASON
I CAN'T DO THIS TODAY.

But examine everything carefully; hold fast to that which is good.
1 THESSALONIANS 5:21

How does this passage apply to your current to-do?

JUSTIFICATION QUESTIONS

1. What are you supposed to be doing?

2. Why do you feel like there's a good reason not to do that right now? Be specific.

3. Is that really a good reason for not working on this to-do? Why or why not?

a. Yes: If so, is there anything you can do now to make it easier to get back to work later? Go ahead and do that and enjoy the time off. You don't need to answer the rest of these questions.

b. No: Is it always convenient to work on goals (or to-dos)? What will you have to give up to work on your goal (or to-do) today?

4. What will you gain if you work on your goal or to-do, even when it's hard?

5. When you think of what you'll gain, is it worth the sacrifice?

6. What do you think God wants to teach you through this trial?

7. What can you thank God for in this situation?

I'LL DO IT LATER.

Whether it is pleasant or unpleasant, we will listen to the voice of the Lord our God.

JEREMIAH 42:6B

How does this passage apply to your current to-do?

PROCRASTINATION QUESTIONS

1. What would you like to accomplish? Be specific.

2. Why don't you want to work on it right now?

3. Based on past experience, what usually happens when you tell yourself you'll do a job later?

4. If you put this off now, when do you think you'll end up doing it? (Be honest.)

5. In the long run, is the procrastination life the good life? Why or why not?

6. If you want to finish this job, will you eventually have to make the sacrifice to work on it?

7. What would you gain by doing it right now?

8. What's the first thing you need to do if you want to work on this project? (Example: Get out your notebook, open the computer file, look up the telephone number, etc.)

9. Why don't you do that right now and see how it goes from there?

I DON'T HAVE TIME.
(EXTREME VERSION)

Look carefully then how you walk, not as unwise but as wise, making the best use of the time, because the days are evil. Therefor do not be foolish, but understand what the will of the Lord is.

EPHESIANS 5:15-17

How does this passage apply to your current to-do?

LACK OF TIME (EXTREME VERSION) QUESTIONS

1. Is there anything special going on in your life right now that's keeping you from spending time on your goal (or current to-do)?

   a. Yes: If so, do you think God wants you to put your goal off until later? Why or why not?

   b. No: If not, continue on with the questions.

2. In the past 48 hours, how much time have you spent in the following activities? Be specific.

   a. Facebook

   b. YouTube

   c. Television

   d. Texting

   e. Computer games

   f. Hobbies

   g. Recreational activities

   h. Hanging out with friends

   i. Surfing the Internet

   j. Exercise

   k. Reading

   l. Talking on the phone

   m. Wandering around your house or apartment

   n. Work that isn't required to support you or your family

3. Would it be possible to make some time for your goal by cutting down on some of your other activities?

GLORIFYING GOD WITH
YOUR TO-DO LIST

Whether, then, you eat or drink or whatever you do, do all to the glory of God.
1 CORINTHIANS *10:31*

Spend some time meditating on 1 Corinthians 10:31, then answer the following questions with today's dreaded to-do in mind.

1. How does this passage apply to your current to-do?

2. Often we make up excuses to not work on our to-do lists just because we don't want to work on them, but sometimes there's a valid reason to not work on them. Think of your day today, how can you glorify God best—by working on your to-do list or not working on it? Explain.

3. What would it look like to live this day for the glory of God?

LOVING OTHERS THROUGH
YOUR TO-DO LIST

Therefore be imitators of God, as beloved children; and walk in love, just as Christ also loved you and gave Himself up for us, an offering and a sacrifice to God as a fragrant aroma. ... Therefore be careful how you walk, not as unwise men but as wise, making the most of your time, because the days are evil.
EPHESIANS 5:1–2, 15–16

Spend some time meditating on Ephesians 5:1–2 and Ephesians 5:15–16, then answer the following questions with today's dreaded to-do in mind.

1. How does this passage apply to your current to-do?

2. How could you make the most of your time today in regard to this task?

3. When you work on this task, who are you loving and how are you loving them?

4. How can you be an imitator of God today and walk in love even if you don't feel like working?

THIS IS NO FUN. I'D RATHER DO SOMETHING ELSE.

But I will sacrifice to You with the voice of thanksgiving.
JONAH 2:9A

How does this passage apply to your current to-do?

INDULGENCE QUESTIONS

1. What would you like to accomplish today? Be specific.

2. Why do you want to accomplish that?

3. What do you feel like doing instead?

4. On a scale of 1 to 10, how satisfying do you think that would be? Explain.

5. In the past, have you been able to do what you feel like doing and still accomplish your goals? Why or why not?

6. What are the advantages of working on your goal (to-do list), even when you don't feel like working on it?

7. Are goals easy to accomplish, or do you usually have to give up something to accomplish them?

8. What will you need to give up to accomplish your goal (or follow your list) this time?

9. When you think of all you'll accomplish, is it worth the sacrifice?

I REALLY DON'T WANT TO DO THIS.

O God, You are awesome from Your sanctuary. The God of Israel Himself
gives strength and power to the people. Blessed be God!

PSALM 68:35

How does this passage apply to your current to-do?

DREAD QUESTIONS

1. What would you like to accomplish today? Be specific.

2. Why do you want to accomplish that?

3. Why don't you feel like working right now?

4. What do you feel like doing instead?

5. If you ignore your project and do that instead, how will you feel afterwards?

6. What will you have to sacrifice to work on your project?

7. How will you feel when you complete this project and why will you feel that way?

8. When you think of how you'll feel, is it worth the sacrifice to work on it? What's the first thing you need to do if you want to work on this project? (Example: Get out your notebook, open the computer file, look up the telephone number, etc.)

9. Why don't you do that right now and see how it goes from there?

THIS IS SO BORING.
I DON'T WANT TO DO IT.

Not that I speak from want, for I have learned to be content in whatever circumstances I am.
PHILIPPIANS 4:11

How does this passage apply to your current to-do?

BOREDOM QUESTIONS

1. If real life were like a romantic comedy or an action thriller, what percentage of your life would be exciting?

2. What percentage of the average person's life is exciting?

3. Think of all the believers in the Bible. What percentage of their lives was fun and exciting?

4. Do you think you have unrealistic expectations for life? Explain.

5. If your main goal in life was to have fun, what would you do with your time right now?

6. What do you think God wants you to do with your time right now?

7. Why do you think He wants you to do that?

8. Are you willing to be bored for God and others if that's what you need to do to love them well?

9. Is there anything you need to accept about life?

10. What can you thank God for in this situation?

I SHOULDN'T HAVE TO DO THIS.
I'VE ALREADY DONE ENOUGH.

Whatever you do in word or deed, do all in the name of the Lord Jesus,
giving thanks through Him to God the Father.
COLOSSIANS 3:17

How does this passage apply to your current to-do?

ENTITLEMENT QUESTIONS

1. Why do you feel like you shouldn't have to work on your goal (habit, list) right now?

2. Why do you feel like you *should* work on it right now?

3. Do you think God wants you to work on your goal (habit, list) right now? Why or why not?

a. Yes: If so, what sacrifices will you have to make to do what God wants you to do? Do you love Him enough to make those sacrifices?

b. No: If not, what do you think God wants you to do instead? Why don't you skip the rest of these questions and go do that?

c. God doesn't care: Would you rather do something else or accomplish your goal, knowing that you can't do both?

4. Is it possible to accomplish this goal (or develop this habit) without ever making any sacrifices for it?

5. What are the advantages of accomplishing this goal (or developing this habit)? List as many as possible.

6. When you think of all the advantages, is it worth the sacrifice to work on it?

DOING YOUR TO-DO LIST
WITH A SERVANT'S HEART

Calling them to Himself, Jesus said to them, "You know that those who are recognized as rulers of the Gentiles lord it over them; and their great men exercise authority over them. But it is not this way among you, but whoever wishes to become great among you shall be your servant; and whoever wishes to be first among you shall be slave of all. For even the Son of Man did not come to be served, but to serve, and to give His life a ransom for many."

MARK 10:42–45

Spend some time meditating on Mark 10:42–45, then answer the following questions with today's dreaded to-do in mind.

1. How does this passage apply to your current to-do?

2. In what ways is the life of a servant boring or even painful?

3. Why do you think Jesus came to serve when He could have been more like the Gentile rulers, lording it over everyone?

4. Why do you think Jesus asks us to serve?

5. Think of your current dreaded to-do. What would it look like to work on this to-do with a servant's heart?

DIFFICULT TO-DOS

All discipline for the moment seems not to be joyful, but sorrowful; yet to those who have been trained by it, afterwards it yields the peaceful fruit of righteousness.

HEBREWS 12:11

Spend some time meditating on Hebrews 12:11, then answer the following questions with today's dreaded to-do in mind.

1. How does this passage apply to your current to-do?

2. What part of doing your project or task is the most sorrowful to you?

3. Why do you think it's so sorrowful?

4. Can you think of any lessons God might want to teach you through your work on this task?

5. According to the author of Hebrews, what's the prize at the end of the training, and what would that look like in this particular situation?

SERVING ONE ANOTHER IN LOVE

For you were called to freedom, brethren; only do not turn your freedom
into an opportunity for the flesh, but through love serve one another.
GALATIANS 5:13

Spend some time meditating on Galatians 5:13, then answer the following questions with today's dreaded to-do in mind.

1. How does this passage apply to your current to-do?

2. What would it look like to use your freedom to indulge your flesh with this particular to-do?

3. What would it look like to use your freedom to serve one another in love?

JESUS VS. OUR FLESH

But put on the Lord Jesus Christ, and make no provision for the flesh in regard to its lusts.
ROMANS 13:14

Spend some time meditating on Romans 13:14, then answer the following questions with today's dreaded to-do in mind.

1. How does this passage apply to your current to-do?

2. What does your flesh want to do today? Be specific.

3. What do you think God wants you to do today?

4. What would be the advantage of doing the things God wants you to do?

WORK THAT PROFITS

All things are lawful for me, but not all things are profitable.
All things are lawful for me, but I will not be mastered by anything.
1 CORINTHIANS 6:12

Spend some time meditating on 1 Corinthians 6:12, then answer the following questions with today's dreaded to-do in mind.

1. How does this passage apply to your current to-do?

2. Do you have the freedom to either work on your to-do list or not work on it today?

3. Would it be profitable to work on it? If so, who would profit and how would they profit?

4. When you think of all who would profit by you working on your to-do list, is it worth working on it?

THIS IS TOO HARD. I CAN'T DO IT.
WHO AM I KIDDING?

Behold, I am the Lord, the God of all flesh; is anything too difficult for me? Ah Lord God!
Behold, You have made the heavens and the earth by Your great power and by
your outstretched arm! Nothing is too difficult for you.
JEREMIAH 32:27, 17

How does this passage apply to your current to-do?

LACK OF CONFIDENCE QUESTIONS

1. What would you like to do?

2. Why do you want to do that?

3. Are you one of those rare (or possibly non-existent) people who can do this effortlessly and perfectly right from the beginning? If not, what's the sad truth you'll have to accept?

4. Has God given you any gifts, talents, or character traits that will make it easier to reach your goal? If so, what are they?

5. What will you need to do if you want to reach your goal? Be specific.

6. Will you have to do that alone, or do you think God would be willing to help? Explain.

7. What do you think God wants to teach you through this trial?

8. What will you gain if you turn to Him for help with this project?

9. What will you gain if you procrastinate, obsess, or turn to a bad habit for "help" with this project?

10. Do you want that to happen?

11. If not, what do you need to do to protect yourself?

12. What is the first task you need to do to get this project going? Be specific. (Example: Get out your notebook, open the computer file, look up the telephone number, etc.)

13. Why don't you do that right now and see how it goes from there?

I'VE ALREADY FAILED AT THIS TODAY. I MIGHT AS WELL GIVE UP.

Do not call to mind the former things, or ponder things of the past.
Behold, I will do something new, now it will spring forth; will you not be aware of it?
I will even make a roadway in the wilderness, rivers in the desert.

ISAIAH 43:18-19

How does this passage apply to today's progress on your to-do list?

Note: Today's questions and the next set of questions (disappointment) could be done when you're already well into the day and haven't even started your to-do list yet. On those days we're tempted to give up but these questions will help you get back on track with your to-do list.

FAILURE QUESTIONS

1. Is it possible to follow your plan (to-do list) perfectly every single day? Why or why not?

2. Why do you think you got off track today?

3. Since you can't go back and change the past, what do you think God wants you to do now?

   a. Be an all or nothing person. If you can't follow your plan perfectly, don't follow it at all.

   b. Beat yourself up and think about what a loser you are.

   c. Keep telling yourself, "You should follow your plan!" Then ignore yourself and go do something else.

   d. Do something else worthwhile that's *not* on the list so that at least you won't feel quite so guilty.

   e. Recognize that things don't always go as expected. Accept the fact that you got sidetracked. Remember that life is about loving God and others, not about performing perfectly. Get back to work on your list/goal, thanking Him that you still have time to work on it.

4. What would be the advantage of continuing to work on your goal (list) even if things haven't gone as smoothly as you wanted them to go?

5. When you think of what you'll gain, is it worth the sacrifice to follow your plan (list) the rest of the day?

6. What can you thank God for in this situation?

THIS ISN'T GOING AS WELL AS I THOUGHT. IS IT WORTH IT?

Be anxious for nothing, but in everything by prayer and supplication with thanksgiving let your requests be made known to God. And the peace of God, which surpasses all comprehension, will guard your hearts and your minds in Christ Jesus.

PHILIPPIANS 4:6-7

How does this passage apply to your current to-do or goal?

DISAPPOINTMENT QUESTIONS

Note: You could use the following questions with your task or to-do list in mind or with the whole goal of overcoming procrastination in mind.

1. What were you expecting to gain/accomplish/achieve?

2. What happened instead?

3. Based on your past experiences with projects and goals, does success usually come in a nice, neat, always-moving-upward curve? If not, how does it usually come?

4. Do you think this is just a minor setback, or is it the death of your project? Explain.

5. What will you need to do if you want to be successful with this project?

6. What do you think God wants to teach you through this trial?

7. Is there anything you need to accept?

8. Is there anything you need to trust God with?

9. What can you thank God for in this situation?

RUNNING WITH ENDURANCE

Therefore, since we have so great a cloud of witnesses surrounding us, let us also lay aside every encumbrance and the sin which so easily entangles us, and let us run with endurance the race that is set before us, fixing our eyes on Jesus, the author and perfecter of faith, who for the joy set before Him endured the cross, despising the shame, and has sat down at the right hand of the throne of God.

HEBREWS 12:1–2

Spend some time meditating on Hebrews 12:1–2, then answer the following questions with today's dreaded to-do in mind.

1. How does this passage apply to your current to-do?

2. What does it look like to run a race with endurance?

3. What would it look like to work on your to-do list with endurance?

4. Read the Scripture again with your own dreaded to-do in mind. What will you need to do if you want to be successful with your "race"?

5. Spend some time visiting with Jesus about your to-do, laying aside any sins or weights that are slowing you down and shifting your focus to Jesus.

LEANING ON GOD
WHEN WORK IS HARD

Hear my cry, O God; give heed to my prayer. From the end of the earth I call to You when my heart is faint; lead me to the rock that is higher than I. For You have been a refuge for me, a tower of strength against the enemy. Let me dwell in Your tent forever; let me take refuge in the shelter of Your wings. Selah.

PSALM 61:1–4

1. Spend some time meditating on Psalm 61:1-4. How does this passage apply to your current to-do?

2. Use Psalm 61:1–4 as a guide for a conversation with God, writing it as you would write it if you were going to God for help. For example, in verse 2 you could say, "From my living room I call to you because I have so much to do and I feel like I can't do it all. Lead me to the Rock that is higher than I! Let me shelter in your presence, high up on the rock, for You are a refuge to me on this crazy day!"

WORKING WITH GOD
VS. WORKING WITHOUT GOD

I can do all things through Him who strengthens me.
PHILIPPIANS 4:13

Spend some time meditating on Philippians 4:13, then answer the following questions with today's dreaded to-do in mind.

1. How does this passage apply to your current to-do?

2. Think of your project today. What would it look like to work on it *without* Christ?

3. What would it look like to work on it *with* Jesus?

4. Would it be easier to do this task if you took some time right not to talk it over with God? If so, go ahead and do that and then get started on your task.

I HAVE TOO MUCH TO DO TODAY.

But as for me, I shall sing of Your strength; yes, I shall joyfully sing of Your lovingkindness in the morning, for You have been my stronghold and a refuge in the day of my distress. O my strength, I will sing praises to You; for God is my stronghold, the God who shows me lovingkindness.

PSALM 59:16-17

How does this passage apply to all you feel you need to get done today?

BEGINNING-OF-WORKDAY STRESS QUESTIONS

Note: I debated about including these questions in the book since you're essentially doing part of this exercise every day when you make your to-do list. I decided to include them, though, just because I think they're helpful to sort through all your jobs when you're overwhelmed.

1. Why are you so stressed today?

2. Can you make a list of all the things you need to get done? If so, go ahead and do that on another piece of paper.

3. Are you able to accomplish everything on your list today?

   a. Yes: If so, why are you feeling so stressed? Consider doing a different set of questions depending on your answer to this question. (Note: My *I Deserve a Donut* app has other questions that may be helpful.)

   b. No: Is there anything you need to accept?

4. Of all the things on your list:

   a. What two things are you dreading the most? Why are you dreading them?

   b. What two things are the most important?

   c. Is there anything you absolutely need to get done today?

d. Is there anything God wants you to do today that's not even on your list?

5. Looking back over your answers to the last question, make a prioritized, realistic list for the day.

6. How can you love God and others best as you work on your list today?

7. If life is about loving God and others, will it be the end of the world if you don't finish your list today?

THIS HAS TO BE PERFECT!

And He has said to me, "My grace is sufficient for you, for power is perfected in weakness." Most gladly, therefore, I will rather boast about my weaknesses, so that the power of Christ may dwell in me.

2 CORINTHIANS 12:9

How does this passage apply to your current to-do?

PERFECTIONISM QUESTIONS

1. What are you trying to do perfectly?

2. What would perfection look like in this case? (Give a thorough description.)

3. Are you capable of making that happen? (Be realistic.)

4. Why do you feel like you have to be perfect?

5. Are you believing any lies? If so, what's the truth for each lie?

6. Does God think you have to be perfect? Why or why not?

7. How is your perfectionism affecting the following:

   a. Your project or habit

   b. Your relationship with God

   c. Your relationship with others

   d. Your health

e. Your personal well-being

8. Is your pursuit of "perfect" worth the sacrifice? Why or why not?

9. What would it look like to pursue this goal as a non-perfectionist?

10. Would you like to pursue this goal as a non-perfectionist? Why or why not?

11. Is there anything you need to accept?

12. What can you thank God for in this situation?

I'LL NEVER BE ABLE TO
GET THIS DONE IN TIME!

Come to Me, all who are weary and heavy-laden, and I will give you rest.
Take My yoke upon you and learn from Me, for I am gentle and humble in heart,
and you will find rest for your souls. For My yoke is easy and My burden is light.

MATTHEW 11:28-30

How does this passage apply to your current to-do or goal?

END OF DAY STRESS QUESTIONS (CAN ALSO USE AT BEGINNING OF DAY!)

1. What do you want to accomplish, and when do you want to accomplish it by?

2. Is that possible? Why or why not?

a. Yes: If so, do you think God wants you to work on that? Why or why not? (If you don't think He wants you to work on it, go on to #2b. If you do think He wants you to work on it, go to #6.)

b. No: If not, what would be the next best option?

    i. **Quit.** If you can't do it on your terms, don't do anything.

    ii. **Stress.** Keep demanding the impossible even though it's driving you (and possibly others) crazy.

    iii. **Hire it out.** Hire someone to do the work so you can finish it on time.

    iv. **Lower your standards.** Keep the current target date but lower your standards and expectations so you can finish it on time without stress.

    v. **Change the target date.** Keep your high standards but change the target date so you have a goal you can actually accomplish.

3. What would be the best thing to do, and why do you think that's best?

4. What will you have to sacrifice or accept if you choose that option?

5. What will you gain if you choose that option?

6. Are there any activities you need to let go of so you have more time to work on this goal? Explain.

7. Is there anything you need to trust God with?

8. What can you thank God for in this situation?

I SHOULD BE WORKING. I NEED TO BE WORKING. I CAN'T STOP WORKING.

Therefore if you have been raised up with Christ, keep seeking the things above, where Christ is, seated at the right hand of God. Set your mind on the things above, not on the things that are on earth. For you have died and your life is hidden with Christ in God.

COLOSSIANS 3:1-3

How does this passage apply to your current desire to keep working?

WORKAHOLISM QUESTIONS

1. Why do you feel like you should work right now?

2. Why do you feel like you shouldn't work right now?

3. Do you think God wants you to work right now? Why or why not?

4. If not, what sacrifices will you have to make to do what God wants you to do?

5. Is it worth doing what God wants you to do even if it's inconvenient or costly? Why or why not?

6. List the advantages of taking a break from both work and thinking about work for awhile.

7. When you think of the advantages, in terms of both life and your relationship with God, is it really that much of a sacrifice to take a break from work?

WHEN YOUR TO-DO LIST
IS STRESSING YOU OUT

*But the Lord answered and said to her, "Martha, Martha, you are worried and
bothered about so many things; but only one thing is necessary, for Mary has chosen
the good part, which shall not be taken away from her."*

LUKE 10:41-42

Spend some time meditating on Luke 10:41–42, then answer the following questions with today's dreaded
to-do in mind.

1. How does this passage apply to your current to-do?

2. Why do you think Martha was so agitated? (See Luke 10:38-40 for context.)

3. Are you agitated about any of your projects, chores, or responsibilities? If so, what makes that project
   so stressful?

4. What implied advice did Jesus give to Martha when she was stressed out about dinner preparations?

5. Sometimes we get stressed because we're expecting far too much from others or ourselves. Other times we get stressed because we're expecting everything to turn out perfectly when that pretty much never happens. Do you have unrealistic expectations for yourself, others, or your project concerning this to-do? If so, spend some time talking to Jesus and letting go of any unrealistic expectations.

WHAT IF I FAIL? (OR WHAT IF THIS IS SUPER HARD, UNCOMFORTABLE, OR BORING?)

"For I know the plans I have for you," declares the Lord, "plans for welfare and not for calamity to give you a future and a hope."

JEREMIAH 29:11

How does this passage apply to your current to-do or goal?

Note: If you're not working on a scary or difficult goal, these questions might not apply. Instead, answer the first question below with "a fun and easy life" or "to stay in my comfort zone" or "a conflict-free life," and answer the questions with that goal in mind. You can also use the worry questions from my *I Deserve a Donut* app to renew your mind for fear.

FEAR OF FAILURE QUESTIONS

1. What would you like to accomplish?

2. What are the odds of you being able to accomplish that? Explain.

3. Why do you want to accomplish that goal?

4. Do you think God also wants you to achieve that goal?

   a. Yes: If so, why does He want you to accomplish it?

   b. No: If not, what does He want?

5. Are God's priorities different than yours? Explain.

6. What are you most afraid of?

7. Why are you afraid of that?

8. Are you coming from a place of being filled up with God and finding your worth in Him? If not, what do you think you have to have to be happy and worthy (success, approval of others, security, status, wealth, etc.)?

9. Would God agree with you? If not, what would He say?

10. What can you thank God for in this situation?

11. Is there anything you need to accept?

WILL THIS BE WORTH ALL THE WORK?
I HAVE TO SUCCEED.

Do not work for the food which perishes, but for the food which endures to eternal life,
which the Son of Man will give to you, for on Him the Father, God, has set His seal.

JOHN 6:27

How does this passage apply to your current to-do or goal?

REWARD/OBSESSION QUESTIONS

1. What is your goal?

2. What will you need to do to accomplish your goal? Be specific.

3. How would you define success with this project?

4. Is it a given that if you do what you need to do, you'll be successful? Why or why not?

5. If you decide to pursue this project, what will you need to accept?

6. Do you think God wants you to work on this project? Why or why not?

7. How do you think He would define success with this project?

8. Is God's definition of success easier to achieve than yours? Why or why not?

9. What would be the advantage of going to God for help with this project, including going to Him for help to see the project through His eyes?

10. Which would be a better reward: 1) intense fellowship with God as you go to Him for help and keep Him (rather than the project) first in your life or 2) money, recognition, and/or worldly success with the project? Explain.

11. What sacrifices will you have to make to get the better reward?

12. Are God's lessons and love in the midst of a trial a reward in and of themselves?

13. What can you thank God for in this situation?

I DON'T KNOW WHAT TO DO
SO I'LL DO NOTHING.

And we know that God causes all things to work together for good to those
who love God, to those who are called according to His purpose.

ROMANS 8:28

How does this passage apply to your current to-do or decision?

DECISION QUESTIONS

1. Why are you having a hard time making this decision?

2. What are your options?

3. Do you have enough information to make a good decision? If not, what information do you need to gather?

4. What do others you respect think about your options?

5. Are you tempted to do something just because it's expected of you? If so, do you also think it's a good thing to do? Why or why not?

6. Does the Bible speak at all to your decision?

   a. Yes: If so, what does it say? Are you willing to do what the Bible says even if you have to sacrifice to do it?

   b. No: If not, does God give you the freedom to make your own decision?

7. Do you think God would prefer one choice over another? If so, why?

8. How will you know if you've made a good decision? (Remember, the idea that you should expect everything in life to go smoothly is a modern concept, not a biblical concept.)

9. Is this one of those situations where you can't really know what's best?

10. What's the worst thing that can happen if you make what appears to be the wrong decision?

11. Can God redeem bad decisions?

12. What will have to sacrifice or accept to make this decision and not keep second-guessing yourself?

13. What can you thank God for in this situation? (Once you make your decision, focus on being thankful for the good things about the option you chose.)

HOLDING "SUCCESS" WITH OPEN HANDS

Though the fig tree should not blossom and there be no fruit on the vines, though the yield of the olive should fail and the fields produce no food, though the flock should be cut off from the fold and there be no cattle in the stalls, yet I will exult in the Lord, I will rejoice in the God of my salvation. The Lord God is my strength, and He has made my feet like hinds' feet, and makes me walk on my high places.

HABAKKUK 3:17–19

Spend some time meditating on Habakkuk 3:17-19, then answer the following questions with today's dreaded to-do in mind.

1. How does this passage apply to your current to-do?

2. Often when we work on a project, we feel as though it has to be successful or it's not worth our efforts. Yet God wants us to hold "success" with open hands. Habakkuk does that in this passage. Personalize this passage by writing out your own fears in verse 17. Then write out verses 18-19 as is, beginning with "yet I will exult in the Lord." For example, you might say, "Though my project turns out terrible and no one likes it and I waste all kinds of money on it with nothing to show for my effort, yet I will exult in the Lord." When you're through writing it, spend some time praying and giving the outcome of your project to God. Remember, He is enough even if your project doesn't turn out!

TRUTH JOURNALING: PROCRASTINATION LIES AND TRUTHS

Another way to renew your mind is what I call truth journaling. With truth journaling, you write down your thoughts, then bring them captive to the truth (2 Corinthians 10:3-5) by recording the truth for each lie. Truth actually changes our desires and makes us want to do those dreaded items on our to-do list—or at least not mind doing them.

Following are ten common lies that make us procrastinate. Circle any of the lies you're believing that make you not want to work on your to-do list today, then record the truth for each lie below. Try to truth journal at least three lies. If you have a hard time coming up with the truth, check out "Procrastination Lies and Truth" on page 161 to see what I wrote for the truths.

1. It's too hard.

2. I can't do it.

3. I don't have time to do it.

4. I will never be able to please _____, so I might as well not even try.

5. I can't do it perfectly, so I might as well not even try.

6. It's better not to try at all than to try and fail.

7. I don't want to do it (and that's a good reason not to do it).

8. I'll do it later.

9. I'll feel more like doing it later, so I'll wait until I feel like doing it.

10. I work best under pressure.

TRUTH JOURNALING:
PERFECTIONISM LIES AND TRUTHS

Review the directions for truth journaling in the previous truth journaling exercise, then circle any of the thoughts below that are making you not want to work on your to-do list today. Record the truth for at least three of the lies you're believing. If you have a hard time coming up with the truth, check out "Perfectionism Lies and Truth" on page 163 to see what I wrote for the truths.

1. This has to be perfect to be acceptable.

2. I'm a failure because I (failed in some way).

3. I can't start this project until (the rest of my life is in order, I know exactly how to do it, I have a large block of time available for it, etc.).

4. If it can't be done well, it's not worth doing.

5. If I'm perfect, people will love me, admire me, accept me, etc. If I mess up, they'll be mad at me.

6. It's terrible if I make a mistake.

7. People expect that of me. I need to live up to their expectations.

8. If I want something done right, I need to do it myself.

9. I'm a bad Christian if (I don't go on a short-term missions trip, I'm not a bubbly person, I don't lead a Bible study, I'm not perfect, etc.).

10. I should have known better.

TRUTH JOURNALING: GENERAL

In the previous truth journaling exercises, you had a list of lies to choose from. This time, try to come up with your own lies. Ask yourself, "What am I believing that's making me not want to do this habit or task on my list?" Record your thoughts below, then list a truth for each lie. If you need a jump start, review the previous two truth journaling exercises. Review the first truth journaling exercise in this book if you need instructions for truth journaling.

LIES

1.

2.

3.

TRUTHS

1.

2.

3.

BENEFITS AND CONSEQUENCES CHART

Another way to renew your mind is with a Benefits and Consequences Chart. Think of the task you don't feel like doing. What are the benefits of putting off that task until later? What are the consequences? Fill in the chart below with that particular task in mind. Don't worry if one side has more entries.

Benefits of Procrastinating	Consequences of Procrastinating

What did you learn from filling out the chart?

END-OF-DAY WORK DETOX

Use these questions at the end of each day to process the day's to-dos if you're feeling stressed. I keep these questions in the Notes section of my phone and go through them at the end of most workdays to help me not think about work at night.

1. What did you get done today?

2. What did you do well today?

3. What could you have done better today?

4. What do you need to remember to do tomorrow? (Do you want to make a list for tomorrow?)

5. Are you believing any lies? If so, what's the truth to each lie?

6. What will you need to accept to stop thinking about work tonight?

7. Do you think God wants you to accept that? Why or why not?

8. What will you do for refreshment and nourishment tonight?

9. What will you do with your computer and phone so you can have fun? (I ask this question to remind myself to put them both away, so I don't waste time on them in the evening!)

RESOURCES

WHAT IS A RENEWING OF THE MIND PROJECT BIBLE STUDY?

The Renewing of the Mind Project is a book I wrote several years ago about going to God for help with our habits, goals, and emotions. The book is based on Romans 12:2 which tells us we're transformed by the renewing of the mind. In the book, I encouraged readers to choose an area of their lives they wanted to change, then renew their minds regularly so they could see transformation.

When I wrote the book, I thought it would be helpful to have workbooks to go with it because I knew from experience how difficult it is to get started on a new "project." Not only do we have our natural procrastinating tendencies to fight, but if we're working on changing something God wants us to change, we also have spiritual warfare to contend with. It would be nice, I thought, to have workbooks geared to specific projects (such as breaking free from insecurity, worry, or procrastination) to help us ease into a project with some guided help.

This is the first of those workbooks. Each workbook will be self-contained (you don't need a copy of *The Renewing of the Mind Project* to do this study) and filled with both Bible studies and opportunities to renew your mind.

I talked about several different ways to renew your mind in *The Renewing of the Mind Project*, such as Scripture meditation, truth journaling, and conversations with God about the area you're trying to change. To make those conversations easier, I included 48 sets of questions to use as a structure for conversations with God. You'll find many of those sets of questions in the Table of Contents of *Freedom from Procrastination*, along with Scripture meditations and truth journaling opportunities. The Scripture meditations will have a title—such as "Glorifying God with Your To-Do List"—and the questions will have a thought, such as "I'll do it later."

When I'm answering the questions myself, I'll often take breaks to talk to God whenever I learn a big truth, but other times I'll just have a conversation with Him during the whole process.

My desire for these workbooks is that you'll see transformation as you go through them. It won't be 100% transformation, but it will be a start. In my own experience of renewing my mind consistently since 2000, I've found that God makes huge changes, but He doesn't completely take away my tendencies toward sin in whatever area I'm working on. What happens is that we'll struggle with that area less often and with less intensity. It goes from something that controls our lives to something that's a minor struggle.

The exciting thing is that we really can change—but transformation comes with a cost. We need to take the time to renew our minds if we want to see change happen. As you renew your mind, remember that if you're a Christian you're doing it from an already-saved position. You're not doing it to earn God's approval—He already accepts you and loves you and cherishes you! So, jump into His arms, nestle against His chest, share your joys and sorrows with Him, and ask Him to give you a biblical perspective on the area of your life you're trying to change. I'm excited to see what He will do in you!

WHAT TO PUT ON YOUR TO-DO LIST

Use these charts to brainstorm things to put on your to-do list. Include things you procrastinate on a regular basis and also things you'd like to get done if you had the time and the oomph. When you're through, remember that it's just a list of ideas. You won't be able to complete all of these things over the course of the study. The first list is for habits and the second list is for tasks. Because habits are so difficult to change, I'd recommend only working on one or two habits over the course of the study.

1. Some of the things we procrastinate have a beginning and an end, such as decluttering a closet. Other things are ongoing, such as doing the dishes after dinner each night. Do you have any habits you'd like to develop that are ongoing? Some examples are processing your mail each day, writing, exercising, or having a quiet time. If so, list those habits, the best time of day to do that habit, and how much time you'd like to devote to the habit each day. Try to stick with daily habits rather than once-a-week habits.

Habit	Best Time of Day for Habit	Time Estimate

2. Set a timer for five minutes and list anything you can think of that you'd like to get done around the house or at work. You could also include things like making doctor's appointments or planning a trip. When you're through making your list, place a check in one of the two columns based on how long the task will take.

Task or Project	Less Than an Hour	More Than an Hour

Don't get discouraged if most of your tasks land in the more than one-hour column. In Week 3, we'll work on breaking those tasks into more manageable chunks using the "Project Lists" on page 157.

SAMPLE TO-DO LIST
AND ACCOUNTABILITY CHART

Note: Go to barbraveling.com/procrastination for a video explanation of how to fill out these charts.

ᴄ Accountability Chart ᴄ

Day	Did you make your list	Was your list realistic based on time estimates?	Did you renew?	How many tasks can you celebrate completing today?
Wednesday	✔	yes	no	1/3
Thursday	✔	✔	✔	3/3
Friday	✔	maybe	✔	2/3
Saturday	no			
Monday	✔	✔	no	1/3
Tuesday	✔	✔	✔	3/3

What did you learn this week?

• If I have an emotionally difficult task that day, I can't plan as much work.

• I am much happier if I wait until 12 p.m. to check social media and even emails!!

Note: Place a check in the renewing column if you renewed your mind with one of the renewing activities in this book before doing any of your tasks. The maximum tasks each day will be three, as it refers to the three tasks on your to-do list. On Wednesday in the above chart, I completed one out of three tasks.

—◌ *To-Do List* ◌—

✓	Day: Wednesday Theme: Procrastination Study	Time Estimate	D or I	Priority
✓	Edit Week 4 study	2 hours	D, I	1
	Research book designers	1 hour	D	2
	Catch up on emails	1 hour	D	3

Note: D is for dread; I is for important. Try to have at least one D every day so you get a chance to go to God for help with procrastination. If you'd like to create a theme for each day, read the Weekly Productivity Tips at the end of Week 4. You can find printable 5-, 6-, and 7-day to-do lists at barbraveling.com/procrastination.

—◌ *Why Only Three To-Dos?* ◌—

More often than not, we don't finish our to-do lists because we're completely unrealistic about how much we can get done in a day. Another problem we have is that we do all the easy tasks first, ignoring the hard to-dos until the end of the day when we're too tired to even think about doing those hard things.

To avoid these hazards, I've asked you to do something that will be hard to do: limit your to-do list to only three items a day. Don't list the things you know you'll do anyway. Instead, list the things you'll have a hard time making yourself do. Often these are the most important things you actually need to do that day.

Before making your list, ask, "What are the three most important things to get done today?" Then estimate the time it will take to do each task. Be realistic about the amount of time each task will take, but also be realistic about the amount of time you have available to work. It's surprising how much time regular life takes—visiting with people, cooking, eating, answering emails, etc. When we add up all of those things, we don't have as much time for non-regular jobs as we think we do.

After making your list, prioritize the tasks based on how important each to-do is and how much you dread doing it, trying to do the worst job first if possible. If you have a hard time thinking of things to put on your to-do list, fill out or review what you wrote on the "What to Put on Your To-do List" charts on pages 152-153.

— ⁓ *If You Work Outside the Home* ⁓—

If you work full-time, try to get in the habit of making a list each day, even if you only have 30 minutes of energy available to work. Just be realistic about how much you think you can accomplish. If you're completely wiped out by the time you get home, you may want to just put a daily habit on the list such as "process today's mail" or "do the dinner dishes" or "go for a walk." If you're a person who feels like you always have to be working, try to put something relaxing on the list such as "take a bath" or "do a puzzle" or "play a game."

PROJECT LISTS

Use these lists to break big and little projects into tasks you can add to your to-do list. You can see an example of this in the second productivity tip at the end of Week 3. Additional project lists can be downloaded at barbraveling.com/procrastination.

Project: _____

Tasks	Time Estimate
1.	
2.	
3.	
4.	
5.	
6.	

Project: _____

Tasks	Time Estimate
1.	
2.	
3.	
4.	
5.	
6.	

Project: _____

Tasks	Time Estimate
1.	
2.	
3.	
4.	
5.	
6.	
7.	
8.	
9.	
10.	

Project: _____

Tasks	Time Estimate
1.	
2.	
3.	
4.	
5.	
6.	
7.	
8.	
9.	
10.	

WEEKLY TO-DO LISTS

Use these lists to plan your top three most important things to get done each week. This list will be more general than your daily to-dos. For example, if one of your goals is to clean the garage and you think you can get it done in a week, place "clean garage" on the list. On the daily list, you'll plan what you think you can accomplish in one day, such as "clean tool bench" or "organize storage closet." I've included these lists in the back of the book so they won't overwhelm you if you're just getting started on overcoming procrastination. If you feel it's too hard mentally or emotionally to come up with a weekly top three, ignore these lists until you're further down the road to overcoming procrastination.

What are the three most important things you'd like to accomplish this week? List them below.

Week One Theme:	Time Estimate	D or I	Priority

What are the three most important things you'd like to accomplish this week? List them below.

Week Two Theme:	Time Estimate	D or I	Priority

What are the three most important things you'd like to accomplish this week? List them below.

Week Three	Theme:	Time Estimate	D or I	Priority

What are the three most important things you'd like to accomplish this week? List them below.

Week Four	Theme:	Time Estimate	D or I	Priority

What are the three most important things you'd like to accomplish this week? List them below.

Week Five	Theme:	Time Estimate	D or I	Priority

PROCRASTINATION LIES AND TRUTHS

Listed below are some common lies that make us procrastinate and some truths that will help you stop procrastinating. They were originally published in *Freedom from Emotional Eating*.

1. It is too hard.

It's hard, but not too hard. I can do hard things. Since it is so hard, I better break it down into more manageable chunks and get started on it right away. I know from experience that the longer I wait to do it, the harder it seems to get in my mind.

2. I can't do it.

I can't do it easily. I can't do it perfectly. But I *can* do it. Also, I can do all things through Him who strengthens me (Philippians 4:13).

3. I don't have time to do it.

This truth will depend on your situation. If you truly don't have time for it, and it isn't important to do it now, then take it off your to-do list. If it's important, the truth is, "I must make time for it." Breaking a big job into smaller jobs may help you fit it into your life more easily.

4. I will never be able to please _____ so I might as well not even try.

It is not my job to please _____. It's my job to please the Lord. If He wants me to do this job, then I need to do it even if I know someone will be critical of how well I do it. If appropriate, I could ask my critical person for input so there is a better chance of the job being approved.

5. I can't do it perfectly, so I might as well not even try.

If this were the way everyone felt, then no one would do anything—because we are all imperfect people! There would be no books to read, no houses to live in, and no movies to go to. The truth is, that of course I can't do it perfectly, so I might as well accept that I can't do it perfectly and just do the best that I can.

6. It's better not to try at all than to try and fail.

Failure is the pathway to success. I can't expect to be good at everything right away. If I learn from my mistakes and don't give up, failure can help me succeed.

7. I don't want to do it (and that's a good reason not to do it).

If God wants me to do it, I should do it whether I want to or not. Also, sometimes I need to do what I don't want to do so I can do what I do want to do.

8. I'll do it later.

90% of the time, when I say I'll do something later, I don't do it. If I want to do it, I better do it right now. The longer I wait, the more I will dread it.

9. I will feel more like doing it later, so I'll wait until I feel like doing it.

In reality, I will probably never feel like doing it.

10. I work best under pressure.

I actually force myself to do it under pressure. This doesn't necessarily mean I do it better. Sometimes, I'm forced to do a poor job because I don't have enough time to do a good job. Often, I am frazzled and grumpy with those around me when I operate this way because I am under *too* much pressure.

PERFECTIONISM LIES AND TRUTHS

Listed below are some common perfectionism lies that make us procrastinate and some truths that will help to stop procrastinating. They were originally published in *Freedom from Emotional Eating*.

1. This has to be perfect to be acceptable.

I can only do my best, and it will never be perfect. Only God is perfect, and He doesn't demand perfection from me. He loves me just as I am.

2. I'm a failure because I (failed in some way).

I'm a sinner saved by grace. I *will* fail from time to time because I'm not perfect. Thankfully, I'm not defined by what I do, but by who I am in Christ. And He doesn't see me as a failure. He sees me as a beloved child of God.

3. I can't start this project until (the rest of my life is in order, I know exactly how to do it, I have a large block of time available for it, etc.).

Chances are, my life will never be in order, I'll never know exactly how to do it, and I'll never have the time to do it the way I want to do it. If I'm going to do it, I must begin now under imperfect conditions.

4. If it can't be done well, it's not worth doing.

I can't learn to do something well until I've done it poorly a few times first. Also, God might want me to do some things to the "pretty good" level so that I have more time to do other things well.

5. If I'm perfect, people will love me, admire me, accept me, etc. If I mess up, they'll be mad at me.

I will never be perfect! They'll have to love me as I am if they're ever going to love me. My job is to love them and ask forgiveness when I sin against them. I can't control what they think of me. And even if they hate me, God will still love me.

6. It's terrible if I make a mistake.

It's *life* if I make mistakes. Everyone else makes them—why should I be exempt?

7. People expect that of me. I need to live up to their expectations.

God wants me to please Him, not others. I am *not required* to live up to the expectations of others. It is *okay* if they're mad at me.

8. If I want something done right, I need to do it myself.

If I want something done *my way*, I need to do it myself. But things don't have to be done my way, and I shouldn't expect others to do things my way. Of course, they will make different decisions, and that is all right. God wants me to be flexible.

9. I'm a bad Christian if (I don't go on a short-term mission trip, I'm not a bubbly person, I don't lead a Bible study, I'm not perfect, etc.).

I am not defined by what I do, but by who I am in Christ. And in Christ, I am a child of my Father, the King of the Universe. A beloved daughter created for the works He wants me to do—not for the works everyone else thinks I should do. As I die to self and live for God, He will be molding me to His image. I am a work-in-progress.

10. I should have known better.

I can't make perfect decisions all the time. Sometimes I'll do the wrong thing, and sometimes I'll make the wrong choice. It's inevitable. But God is sovereign and full of grace. He'll work all things together for good (Romans 8:28).

LEADER'S GUIDE, PROCRASTINATION VIDEOS, AND OTHER RESOURCES

Leader's Guide

Freedom from Procrastination can be done as an individual study or a group study. If you'd like to lead a group study with *Freedom from Procrastination,* you can download a free leader's guide and an introductory video at barbraveling.com/procrastination.

Procrastination Videos and Podcasts

Supplementary videos and podcast episodes with tips on overcoming procrastination are available at barbraveling.com/procrastination.

Printable To-Do Lists and Other Procrastination Resources

Downloadable 5-, 6-, and 7-day to-do lists are available at barbraveling.com/procrastination, along with any other resources mentioned in the book.

Other Books by Barb Raveling

Rally: A Personal Growth Bible Study
Renewing of the Mind Project
Taste for Truth: A 30 Day Weight Loss Bible Study
Freedom from Emotional Eating (Bible Study)
I Deserve a Donut (And Other Lies That Make You Eat)

Apps

I Deserve a Donut is available as both an Android and iPhone app.

Podcasts

Taste for Truth Christian Weight Loss Podcast.

The Christian Habits Podcast.

Website

Barbraveling.com